BOYCOT
ISRA__
IS WRONG

PHILIP MENDES is the Director of the Social Inclusion and Social Policy Research Unit in the Department of Social Work at Monash University. He has been writing about and researching the Israeli-Palestinian conflict for over 30 years, and is the author or co-author of eight books including *The New Left, the Jews and the Vietnam War, 1965-72* (1993), jointly edited with Geoffrey Brahm Levey, *Jews and Australian Politics* (2004), and *Jews and the Left: The rise and fall of a political alliance* (2014).

NICK DYRENFURTH is an Adjunct Research Fellow in the National Centre for Australian Studies at Monash University. He is the author or editor of six books, including *Mateship: A Very Australian History* (2015), *A Little History of the Australian Labor Party* (2011, with Frank Bongiorno), *Heroes and Villains: The rise and fall of the early Australian Labor Party* (2011), and *All That's Left: What Labor should stand for* (2010, edited with Tim Soutphommasane). Nick is a leading media commentator and has also worked as a Labor Party adviser and speechwriter.

BOYCOTTING ISRAEL IS WRONG

THE PROGRESSIVE PATH TO PEACE BETWEEN PALESTINIANS AND ISRAELIS

PHILIP MENDES & NICK DYRENFURTH

NEWSOUTH

A NewSouth book

Published by
NewSouth Publishing
University of New South Wales Press Ltd
University of New South Wales
Sydney NSW 2052
AUSTRALIA
newsouthpublishing.com

National Library of Australia
Cataloguing-in-Publication entry

Creator: Mendes, Philip, 1964– author.
Title: Boycotting Israel is wrong: The progressive path to peace between
Palestinians and Israelis / Philip Mendes, Nick Dyrenfurth.
ISBN: 9781742234144 (paperback)
    9781742242019 (ePub/Kindle)
    9781742247304 (ePDF)
Notes: Includes bibliographical references and index.
Subjects: Arab-Israeli conflict
    Propaganda, Anti-Israeli.
    Palestinian Arabs – Government policy – Israel.
    Israel – Politics and government.
    Palestine – Politics and government.
Other Creators/Contributors: Dyrenfurth, Nick, author.
Dewey Number: 956.94054

Design Josephine Pajor-Markus
Cover design Xou Creative
Printer Griffin Press

Contents

Acknowledgments

Both Nick and Philip are grateful to Phillipa McGuinness, our publisher at NewSouth Publishing. Wading into the debate over a sliver of land between the Jordan River and the Mediterranean Sea involves risks for editors as well as authors. We are also grateful to our editor Averil Moffat for the meticulous care with which she handled our book.

Nick and Philip would also like to thank three colleagues who initially helped develop this project or read this book in draft format: David Hirsh, Andrew Markus and Ralph Seliger. Our book is immeasurably better for their considered criticism and commentary. Any errors of course remain those of the authors. Philip is grateful to a number of people who have helped to inform his perspective on this contentious topic. They include most notably Allan Borowski, Douglas Kirsner, Bill Rubinstein, Suzanne Rutland, Irving Wallach, Peter Wertheim and Uri Windt. He is particularly grateful to his co-author Nick Dyrenfurth for inspiring the idea of this book, and his warm friendship throughout the writing process. As always, his family has been behind him all the way: his cherished wife Tamar

Lewit, his adored children Miranda and Lucas, and his beloved mother Mary. Nick would also like to thank many of the same colleagues and friends who have guided him into these debates. He owes a special debt of gratitude to Philip Mendes for his guidance and friendship. Nick's indefatigable family – Sophy, Micah and Ariella – have put up with several years of frenzied writing on different projects. Their unconditional love and support made it bearable.

Abbreviations

AFL–CIO	American Federation of Labor and Congress of Industrial Organizations
AFP	Australians for Palestine
AJDS	Australian Jewish Democratic Society
AMWU	Australian Manufacturing Workers Union
APAN	Australia Palestine Advocacy Network
ASA	American Studies Association
AUT	Association of University Teachers (UK)
AWU	Australian Workers' Union
BDS	Boycott, Divestment and Sanctions
BRICUP	British Committee for the Universities of Palestine
CFMEU	Construction, Forestry, Mining and Energy Union
CJPP	Coalition for Justice and Peace in Palestine
CPACS	Centre for Peace and Conflict Studies
CUPE	Canadian Union of Public Employees

Abbreviations

EUMC	European Monitoring Centre on Racism and Xenophobia
IAJV	Independent Australian Jewish Voices
IDF	Israeli Defence Forces
ITUC	International Trade Union Confederation
JCCV	Jewish Community Council of Victoria
NATFHE	National Association of Teachers in Further and Higher Education (UK)
NGO	Non-Governmental Organisations
NTEU	National Tertiary Education Union (Aust.)
NUJ	National Union of Journalists (UK)
NUS	National Union of Students (UK)
PACBI	Palestinian Campaign for the Academic and Cultural Boycott of Israel
PGFTU	Palestinian General Federation of Trade Unions
PLO	Palestine Liberation Organization
PSC	Palestine Solidarity Committee (UK)
SDP	Somerville Divestment Project (USA)
SJP	Students for Justice in Palestine
STUC	Scottish Trades Union Congress
TULIP	Trade Unions Linking Israel and Palestine
UCU	University and College Union (UK)

Introduction

A funny thing happened on the way to the March 2011 New South Wales state election. As the Labor government of Kristina Keneally approached its long-awaited date with electoral destiny, Middle East politics moved to the centre stage of a lacklustre contest. A few months earlier, in December 2010, the state conference of the NSW Greens Party had voted to throw its support behind the Boycott, Divestment and Sanctions (BDS) campaign. Citing the 1960s US civil rights movement and the struggle against Apartheid South Africa, then NSW Greens Senator-elect Lee Rhiannon hailed the move. It would 'help bring peace to the people of Israel and Palestine', she declared. 'We hope to build a broad-based campaign in Australia similar to what has been achieved overseas'.[1]

It was a forlorn, if disingenuous hope. Four years later, the tragedy of the Israeli–Palestinian conflict seems no closer to a peaceful, lasting resolution. Nor is a pro-BDS stance the formal policy of the NSW Greens, having been abandoned by the party at its December 2011 state conference. In the intervening period, the issue triggered a tsunami of controversy, embroiling inner-west Sydney's

Marrickville Council in an emotive national debate. In the election's aftermath, commentators credited the defeat of Marrickville Greens candidate Fiona Byrne, who as mayor of the local council sought to implement the BDS as formal policy, to her support for the BDS. Remarkably, however, Rhiannon insisted that her party had erred only by not spending more time building 'progressive support' for the BDS campaign among 'academics, Arab communities and social justice groups'.[2] Party members and supporters of the Greens were shell-shocked by this turn of events. For more seasoned observers, the political vaudeville was hardly surprising.

To boycott, or not to boycott? This is the question that has gripped sections of progressive politics and the trade union movement across much of the West since the BDS campaign was launched a decade ago. BDS advocates claim to be motivated by a concern to alleviate Palestinian suffering, and to end the denial of national rights to Palestinians living inside the Israeli-occupied West Bank. But their analysis of the Israeli–Palestinian conflict is based on a simplistic world view of good and bad nations. This caricature labels the Israelis as nefarious and immoral oppressors, and the Palestinians as defenceless and innocent victims. Hence they construct superficial and false race-based analogies between current Israeli policies and earlier South African apartheid, rather than acknowledging the real complexity of two peoples with equally legitimate national aspirations struggling over one piece of land.

Not surprisingly, the BDS has scarcely assisted the peace process between Israel and the Palestinians. It has clearly failed to realise its stated aims, most importantly ending the Israeli occupation of the West Bank (and East Jerusalem), securing a so-called Right of Return to Israel for Palestinian refugees from the 1948 war, and gaining national as well as civil rights for Arab citizens of Israel. Nor, as Rhiannon hoped, has it morphed into a broad-based campaign in Australia or elsewhere. From the most elite of university campuses to rallies outside chocolate shops or debate on the floor of legislatures, BDS's major 'success' has been to pour fuel on the fires of an already polarised debate.

The Israeli–Palestinian conflict is one of the bitterest and seemingly most intractable of modern times, a history that we chart in terms of the wider trajectory of progressive attitudes towards the national rights of the Jewish people in chapter 1. When the American-sponsored Oslo Peace Process (1993) collapsed in the wake of the failure of the Camp David Summit of 2000 to reach an agreement on final status issues being negotiated between Israeli Prime Minister Ehud Barak and Yasser Arafat's Palestinian Authority – in turn leading to the violent uprising of the Second Intifada[3] – the campaign for BDS against Israel gained momentum as one international solution to the conflict. Its origins lie in the infamous Non-Governmental Organisations (NGO) Forum of the World Conference on Racism staged under the auspices of the United

Nations in Durban, South Africa in September 2001. The NGO Forum rapidly descended into anti-Semitic farce sparking diplomatic walkouts.

The 21st-century boycott Israel movement had made an inauspicious beginning. Indeed, its association with Durban meant that the BDS was effectively stillborn. Four years later, however, a renewed push saw the self-styled Palestinian Campaign for the Academic and Cultural Boycott of Israel (PACBI) officially formed in July 2005, issuing a 'call' for boycotting Israel in the name of 'Palestinian Civil Society'. It was, in the manner of Durban, self-consciously imitative of the African National Congress's call for a boycott of Apartheid South Africa. Yet not only is BDS a rather dubious moral successor, it is perhaps the worst of any of the conflict resolution solutions currently on offer. At its core is a thinly veiled campaign to resuscitate the so-called one-state solution whereby the State of Israel would give way to an Arab-dominated Greater Palestine in which Jews constitute at best a tolerated *religious* minority. Gaza-born Palestinian-American Ahmed Moor, a leading BDS activist, explicitly acknowledges the real agenda. 'Ending the occupation doesn't mean anything if it doesn't mean upending the Jewish state itself', he wrote in 2010, 'BDS does mean the end of the Jewish state.'[4] Genuine peace activists can have no truck with this mindset.

We explore the specific faults of the BDS movement's three major aims in chapter 2. Suffice to say its original sin is a wilful historical ignorance of the conflict's roots. It begins with the claim that Israel's foundation in 1948 was somehow unique. Yet, measured against similar partitions of disputed lands, for instance in the case of India and Pakistan, there wasn't anything unusual about the events that took place in Mandate Palestine during 1947–48. Moreover, Israel was founded in the wake of the Shoah (Holocaust) as a bulwark against anti-Jewish persecution and discrimination that indelibly marked modern history. It rested on the overwhelming understanding among Jews worldwide that they constituted a distinctive ethnic-religious group with national rights to self-determination. It is for this reason that some kind of attachment to Israel is important to the identity of many, if not most, non-Israeli Jews. The designation of Israel as 'apartheid', 'racist' or 'Nazi' – each a common theme in the rhetoric of BDS supporters, Arab or otherwise – sets up an unfair presumption that most Jews are apologists for these beliefs.

Consciously or not, BDS supporters also adopt a blasé attitude to the historical analogies with earlier calls to boycott Jews, whether those of Nazi-era Germany, the Arab League boycott of Israel beginning in 1948, or the less well-known banning of Jewish student societies in the West during the 1970s. By contrast, they have little to say of ongoing Palestinian rejectionism, especially of the racist, religious fundamentalist Hamas variety.

Significantly, BDS supporters seem unconcerned that they may in some way contribute to the growing unease felt by sections of the Jewish diaspora, especially in Europe. Whether it is Greece's neo-Nazi Golden Dawn party, Ukraine's Svoboda, France's National Front or Hungary's Jobbik, far-right and often explicitly anti-Semitic parties are on the march. Numerous violent incidents have taken place over the past several years including the murders of Jewish citizens in Europe by radical Islamists, most recently the killing of four French Jews in Paris. The conflict between Israel and Hamas during July–August 2014 provoked a wave of anti-Semitic outbursts from Europe to Australia. Synagogues and Jewish businesses were attacked. Rallies in Germany and France chanted 'Jews to the gas chambers' and 'Death to the Jews'.[5] BDS is clearly not to blame for these racist outrages, but it scarcely discourages anti-Semitism either.

On the surface, the BDS campaign in the West appears to have achieved some success in terms of isolating Israel, another key, if informal aim of activists who support its mission. The BDS has attracted support from legal experts, academics, literary figures, musicians, artists, churches, trade unions and other non-government organisations. Many eminent and often well-meaning individuals have engaged positively with BDS. The support of respected South African Archbishop Desmond Tutu is frequently cited, hardly surprising given the regular invocation of Israeli apartheid by BDS activists.[6] BDS has certainly attracted the attention of the media, much of which has been unfavourable. Still, no democratic government has endorsed any form of boycott which is crucial both for Israel's international standing and its ability to maintain normal trade relations. Arguably the greatest achievement of the BDS campaign thus far has been the inflammatory contribution of its activists to the tone of an already heated debate.

You can, as we do, believe the ongoing Israeli occupation of the West Bank to be a dangerous folly, and that retention of the West Bank settlements involves a blurring between Israel's legitimate right to self-defence and illegitimate demands for territorial expansion and ethnic domination, and clearly precludes progress towards a viable two-state solution. One can also believe, as we do, that the current Israeli Likud-led coalition government of Binyamin Netanyahu has failed to promote a two-state solution, or deter supporters of the Greater Israel project, who press for a State of Israel that would have sovereignty over all land from the Jordan River to the Mediterranean Sea.

At the same time, many Israelis legitimately fear that any political or territorial concessions on the West Bank will only be used by the Palestinians to initiate further violence, given the prevalence of suicide bombings following the signing of the Oslo Peace Accord and the rocket attacks that followed the Israeli withdrawal from Gaza in 2005. Any negotiated peace solution will necessarily require difficult compromises by both sides that eschew simplistic Greater Israel or Greater Palestine agendas.

In contrast to a peace based on mutual recognition and compromise, the one-sided wrongs of the BDS campaign are legion. BDS singles out only Israel for boycott, ignoring far worse human rights abuses and bitter ethnic-religious conflicts. If anything, Israeli actions are far less brutal than the behaviour of China in Tibet, the United States during Vietnam, Indonesia in Aceh and formerly East Timor, and Russia in Chechnya. This is to say nothing of the persecution of minority racial or religious groups within Zimbabwe, Sudan, Iran, Rwanda and elsewhere. BDS also collectively punishes all Israelis for the actions of their state; it demonises Jews who oppose it; it educates followers that the Jewish state is at the centre of all that is wrong in the world; it puts a campaign against the Jewish state at the top of the agenda of progressive activists; it pushes many Jews out of progressive movements and strengthens the hand of hardliners in Israel allowing them to perpetuate a 'bunker mentality' among sections of the population. In both Western and Arab worlds, BDS recycles images of Jews as bloodthirsty oppressors exercising disproportionate influence; and popularises the specious idea that people who raise the issue of anti-Semitism are doing so in bad faith in order to silence any criticism of the Israeli State.

By portraying Israel as a unique evil, the BDS movement tends to demonise anybody who opposes these methods, most commonly Israelis but also diaspora Jews. One example may suffice. The Histadrut is the General Federation of Labour in Israel, founded in 1920. It is obviously not part of the current Israeli government and has called for an end to settlement construction in the West Bank and for the blockade of Gaza to be lifted. It has a functioning relationship with the Palestinian General Federation of Trade Unions. And yet, according to BDS supporters, this organisation must be boycotted, isolating a progressive movement in Israel and eliminating constructive if imperfect relations with Palestinian civil society. In short, the BDS movement tends to write off an entire people, slamming the door shut on peace.

The BDS campaign is bad for Israelis, bad for Jews and bad for Palestinians. It is also corrosive of progressive movements and civil society. To teach good people that Zionism – at its core the Jewish people's aspiration for national self-determination in their historic homeland – is the first enemy of progress is the antithesis of progressive politics. Indeed, as we shall see, local BDS campaigns have led to numerous manifestations of anti-Semitism within the British tertiary sector, notably from the UK University and College Union (UCU). In October 2014, South African BDS activists placed a pig's head next to kosher products in a Cape Town supermarket of the Woolworths chain.[7] A further example closer to home are outbursts of anti-Jewish hatred on campuses and on social media fostered by supporters of the BDS movement at leading universities in Australia.[8] And despite the denials of the

BDS leadership, individual Israelis and Jews *have* been singled out for boycott, the most dramatic example being the walkout staged by far-left British MP George Galloway during a debate at Oxford University in early 2013. In August 2014, Galloway declared his constituency of Bradford West to be an 'Israel-free zone'.[9]

Most supporters of BDS obviously don't see themselves as anti-Semitic and many are no such thing. Supporters of a limited boycott targeting Israeli settlements in the West Bank even include Zionists, most prominently the American Jewish journalist Peter Beinart, and the American Partners for Progressive Israel (formerly known as Meretz USA).

In our view, BDS advocates are simply not interested in promoting Israeli–Palestinian peace or reconciliation. Nor is their campaign about ending the occupation of the West Bank, or about challenging specific Israeli government policies towards the Palestinians. Rather BDS is a regressive strategy that takes us back to the bad old days that predated the Israeli victory in the 1967 Six-Day War when all Arabs and Palestinians boycotted Israel. Also, to the days prior to the 1993 Oslo Peace Accord when Israel refused to speak with the Palestine Liberation Organization as the leaders of the Palestinian people.

Of course there are many activists around the world who are taking action to promote the national rights of both Israelis and Palestinians. One thinks here of the former Australian Workers' Union national secretary Paul Howes, a key figure, along with British trade union leader Michael Leahy and American trade union leader and President of the Jewish Labor Committee Stuart Appelbaum, in the creation of the Trade Unions Linking Israel and Palestine (TULIP) initiative.[10] In a speech delivered in 2010, Howes argued the case for positive co-operation to promote worker rights and two states. He did not ignore the ongoing occupation. Yet the BDS movement, in Howes's opinion, was an initiative imposed on the Palestinians by outside agitators, who won't have to live with the practical pain a BDS will cause – fewer jobs and lower living standards. And, of course, no Palestinian state.[11] Prominent Palestinians argue as much. Palestinian Authority President Mahmoud Abbas explicitly opposes a blanket boycott of Israel as proposed by the BDS campaign.[12] Sari Nusseibeh, the Palestinian president of Al-Quds University, specifically rejects boycotts of Israeli academics, insisting that they hold 'the most progressive pro-peace views and views that have come out in favor of seeing us as equals'. 'If you want to punish any sector, this is the last one to approach.'[13]

Sadly, much of the debate around BDS has been framed by extremists from both sides of the equation. Perhaps the most well-known book on the subject of Israel-Palestine from an Australian perspective was written by a prominent BDS supporter, left-wing journalist Antony Loewenstein. A supporter of the one-state solution, he starts from the premise that Israel's existence must end. Our book, written by two progressive Jewish opponents of the 'Israel-always-right' lobby, offers an antidote to Loewenstein's 'Israel-always-wrong' polemic. Internationally, several pro-BDS books have been published, including a book authored by Omar Barghouti, a founding member of the campaign to boycott Israel. He was also a contributor to the fiercely anti-Israel collection *The Case for Sanctions against Israel* (2012).[14]

A more scholarly account of the BDS movement is American 'Peace Studies' academic Maia Carter Hallward's *Transnational Activism and the Israeli-Palestinian Conflict* (2013). However, the four case studies upon which she based her findings were limited to the United States. Arguably her book represented a thinly veiled apologia for BDS, albeit shorn of the incendiary language deployed by other advocates. BDS, according to Carter Hallward, was a 'time-tested tool that has worked through-out history'.[15] Yet nowhere in this account of the movement were allegations of anti-Semitism taken seriously. The eliminationist rhetoric and agenda of key BDS advocates – arguing that Israel should cease to exist as a nation state – was simply swept under the carpet. A recent edited book by Cary Nelson and Gabriel Noah Brahm provides an effec-tive critique of the BDS from a range of viewpoints, but is mostly limited to the US debate.[16] There are a number of Left Zionist books addressing the shortcomings of Israeli political culture and the actions of successive governments, such as Gershom Gorenberg's *The Unmaking of Israel* and *Haaretz* journalist Ari Shavit's *My Promised Land*. There are also calls for the Jewish diaspora to speak out against the wrongheaded policies of the Israeli State in order to help end the conflict. In Beinart's *The Crisis of Zionism* he controversially argued for a form of 'Zionist BDS' that specifically targets the products of Israeli West Bank settlements.[17] There are however no works that explain why BDS is clearly wrong and which properly contextualise its origins within the Arab-Israeli conflict and the complex history of Zionism and left-wing politics.

By contrast, this book examines the principal dynamics of the BDS movement in Australia, Europe and the United States. We begin with a broad overview of the conflict, including a discussion of progressive approaches to the Israel–Palestine debate as well as the historical relationship of Jewish activists and Zionism to progressive and labour movement politics since the late 19th century. (The Palestinian-Israeli conflict can be understood as one facet of the conflict between elements of Islam and the West and with modernity more generally, but we do not propose to explore these issues here.) We then critically analyse the key arguments for and against the BDS, before undertaking two case studies, firstly in Australia and the second taking in major developments in Britain and the United States.

In conclusion, we argue that only anti-BDS progressives can lead the way towards a just and peaceful resolution of the conflict through a two-state plan that fosters dialogue and urges mutual compromise and concessions from both sides who are prepared to accept a form of *partial justice* rather than a zero-sum solution, ultimately key to the establishment of two states for both peoples. This genuinely progressive view, based on support for Israel's existence and recognition of Palestinian rights to a homeland, is increasingly excluded from local and international debates. It is a voice that urgently needs to be reheard.

1

The Left, Zionism and Israel, 1897–2014

Debates over the national rights of the Jewish people have exercised thinkers and parties associated with the Left from the mid-19th century onwards.[1] This trend strengthened with the establishment of the State of Israel in 1948. Despite once offering unyielding support, since 1967 the major source of political and ideological hostility to the world's only Jewish state has largely emanated from the Left.

Today, too, most of the Western support for the Boycott, Divestment and Sanctions (BDS) movement also comes from individuals and groups who identify with the political Left. Indeed it is sometimes assumed that there has always been a natural affinity between progressive politics and support for hardline Palestinian nationalism. This view is badly mistaken.

In this opening chapter we show that the Left has always held a wide spectrum of ideas concerning the Zionist ideal, the legitimacy of a Jewish national homeland and the precise means of solving the near-century-long conflict in Israel/Palestine.

To be sure, many progressive groups ridiculed Theodore Herzl's pioneering formation of the Zionist movement in 1897, and strongly opposed Britain's 1917 Balfour Declaration proposing the establishment of a Jewish homeland in Palestine. But equally, many leading Left figures supported both Jewish settlement and the Zionist goal of creating a Jewish state in mandatory Palestine. Later, almost the entire international Left, whether communist or social democratic, supported the creation of Israel in 1948.

Left support for Zionism and Israel has declined significantly since Israel's victory in the 1967 Six-Day War and its ongoing occupation of Palestinian territories. However, today there exists a substantial difference between the majority of Left groups, which favour a two-state solution and reject the West Bank settlement project, and the minority of anti-Zionist fundamentalists who would seek to deny Israel's very existence. As we shall see, it is mainly the latter group who endorse the full agenda of the BDS movement.

Left attitudes to Zionism pre-1948

Prior to World War One, the international socialist movement was not sympathetic to Zionism. Major figures such as Lenin, Stalin and the influential Czech-German Marxist theoretician Karl Kautsky were all strong critics of the Zionist movement. In general terms, this opposition reflected the Left's hostility to any form of distinctive Jewish national or group identity, whether in its Zionist or Bundist (a secular, socialist European movement founded in the late 19th century that emphasised the common culture of the Jewish people and Yiddish language) forms.

Opposition to Zionism existed for a number of reasons. First, from a philosophical point of view, Zionism was viewed as a counter-revolutionary force that allegedly abandoned the struggle for Jewish rights in Europe, and instead ceded victory to right-wing anti-Semites who wished to rid Europe of the so-called 'Jewish question' by forced emigration. By contrast, the Left believed that the global triumph of socialism would end all forms of racial hatred including anti-Semitism.[2]

A second argument reflected self-interest. Most European left-wing groups included a significant number of Jewish members whose activism was seen as vital to the success of the class struggle, whether social democratic or communist in trajectory.

A third, ostensibly practical, argument held that Zionism had little chance of success given the extent of Arab hostility towards a Jewish homeland in their midst and later the perceived perfidy of British imperialism. A review of Herzl's 1896 book *The Jewish State* in the German Socialist press, for example, described the plan to create a Jewish State in Palestine as 'bizarre' and 'utopian'. Another late

19th-century socialist writer dismissed the Zionist project as 'a movement created by a nucleus of romantic intellectuals by which a nation that is no longer living presents itself for the last time on the scene of history before disappearing definitively'.[3]

It should also be remembered that at this time the Zionist movement enjoyed the support of only a small minority of Jews, such as the European activists of the Poale Zion socialist–labour organisation and Herzl's liberal grouping. The chief opposition came from the Jewish Labour Bund centred in Poland which viewed labour Zionism as a potentially significant rival for the allegiance of the Jewish working class. The Bund opposed Zionism as a reactionary diversion from the task of fighting anti-Semitism and defending Jewish rights in the diaspora.[4]

But anti-Zionism was also influential within mainstream Jewish establishment groups, religious (Orthodox and reform) or otherwise secular. Many Jews appear to have regarded Zionism as an extremist movement with utopian, if not politically dangerous, objectives. They feared that support for the creation of a Jewish state in Palestine would provoke dangerous accusations of dual loyalties. Additionally, there were other competing non-territorial Jewish nationalist movements that demanded national autonomy within existing European states.[5] Some religious Jews did not believe in, and remain opposed to, the idea of Jews establishing a form of government in the Land of Israel without the divinely inspired intervention of a Messiah (Moshiach).

Yet even at this early time there was a socialist exception to the anti-Zionist orthodoxy. The source was the *Sozialistische Monatshefte*, the magazine of the German revisionist socialists, which was ideologically opposed to the orthodox Marxism espoused by the leading theoretical journal of German social democracy, *Die Neue Zeit*. This revisionist magazine, which was published by an East Prussian Jew, Josef Bloch, critiqued the Left's assimilationist perspective, recognised Jewish national rights, and published positive reports of Zionist communal settlements in Palestine.[6]

The issuing of the Balfour Declaration in 1917 during World War One and the establishment of the British mandate over Palestine provoked a major increase in Jewish support for the aims of Zionism. It also impacted positively on key sections of the socialist movement, which now viewed Zionism as a practical movement with some prospect of success. Additionally, the horrific pogroms perpetrated upon Eastern European Jews during and immediately following the Bolshevik Revolution of the same year demonstrated to many European socialists that anti-Semitism could not suddenly be eliminated by revolution or cultural assimilation.[7]

To be sure, the Bolsheviks and subsequently the Soviet Union and the Communist International (later known as the Comintern) consistently opposed Zionism on ideological grounds from 1917 until at least the end of World War Two. They denounced the Balfour Declaration and the British mandate in Palestine. But they also displayed some tolerance for Zionist activities inside the Soviet Union until the late 1920s, broadly accepted the legitimacy of Jewish settlement in Palestine, and advocated Jewish-Arab unity within Palestine. It was only following the 1929 Arab riots in Palestine that the Soviets shifted to a clear endorsement of the Arab nationalist agenda. Henceforth the Comintern rejected any distinction between the Jewish community and Zionism, and labelled all Palestinian Jews counter-revolutionary tools of British imperialism.[8]

By contrast, many socialists reconsidered their approach to Zionism. This was particularly the case for those of a revisionist or social democratic stamp. The non-Marxist or social democratic fragment of Poale Zion (which had split during the latter part of World War One) won official recognition from various International Socialist Conferences between 1917 and 1920, and from the Socialist Second International. In addition, leading social democrats such as the Austrians Engelbert Pernerstorfer and Max Adler; the Germans Rudolf Breitscheid, Eduard Bernstein and Paul Loebe; George Lansbury, HN Brailsford, Richard Tawney, Fenner Brockway, Philip Snowden and Bertrand Russell from Britain; the Frenchmen Leon Blum, Charles Gide, Marius Moutet, Vincent Auriol and Jean Longuet; and the Belgians Emile Vandervelde and Camille Huysmans gave their support to the goals of Zionism.

Forty socialists representing eight different countries attended a pro-Zionist international Socialist
conference convened by Poale Zion in 1928. This
conference voted to establish a Socialist Pro-Palestine Committee to assist the activities of the Jewish
labour movement in Palestine.[9]

One of the strongest supporters of pre-World
War Two support for Zionism was the leading Bel-
gian socialist Emile Vandervelde. During his visit to
Tel Aviv in 1928, he proclaimed how the Yishuv had
demonstrated that 'the sun of socialism is beginning
to rise on the world'. He argued that Labour Zionism had made a special contribution to the practical development of socialism due to its agricultural
base, its collective ownership of the land and its
emphasis on avoiding exploitation of other ethnic-
ities.[10] His subsequent book *A Marxist in Palestine*
praised Zionism as 'one of the most wonderful ide-
alistic efforts of our time'.[11]

The British Labour Party was particularly sympathetic to the aims of the Labour Zionist movement.
As early as August 1917, it committed itself to the
formation of a Jewish state in Palestine. Numerous
Labour MPs including Ramsay MacDonald, Arthur
Henderson, Herbert Morrison and Josiah Wedg-
wood visited Palestine and were impressed by Zionist activities. Successive annual party conferences
from 1936 to 1945 supported the establishment of
a Jewish state. The party strongly condemned the
British Government's 1939 White Paper on Palestine, which limited Jewish immigration.[12] In 1944,

the Labour Party Conference voted for the admission of Jews to Palestine 'in such numbers as to become a majority'. The relevant motion, principally drafted by leading party figure Hugh Dalton, stated that 'There was a strong case for this before the War. There is an irresistible case now, after the unspeakable atrocities of the cold and calculated German Nazi plan to kill all Jews in Europe.' The motion also urged the 'transfer' of the Arab population to neighbouring countries.[13]

Nevertheless, this explicitly pro-Zionist position was never implemented. Due to a range of pragmatic military and foreign policy considerations, the British Labour Government from 1945 to 1948 displayed overwhelming hostility to the Zionist campaign for a Jewish state in Palestine. The Foreign Secretary Ernest Bevin attempted to limit Jewish immigration to Palestine and sent the navy to intercept boatloads of Jewish Holocaust survivors and place them in internment camps.[14] However, the party leadership was repeatedly challenged by left-wing MPs and intellectuals such as Harold Laski, Richard Crossman, Aneurin Bevan and Michael Foot who fought for the Party's traditional pro-Zionist objectives. They viewed the Jewish settlement of Palestine as a necessary socialist enterprise, and demanded that the government adopt a position in support of unlimited Jewish immigration leading to partition and the establishment of a Jewish state.[15]

This passionate left-wing support for Zionism

and later Israel was also reflected in most other Western social democratic parties. Many social democrats were impressed by the activities of the Histadrut, the General Federation of Jewish Labour, and various co-operative agricultural settlements – the kibbutzim and the moshavim. In 1945 the prominent Austrian socialist Julius Braunthal wrote a highly positive account of his visit to Palestine during 1938, describing the Jewish labour movement as the equivalent of the famous earlier Austrian labour movement of 'Red Vienna'. Braunthal praised the Histadrut organisation, the workers' health service and the broader socialist Zionist political parties and culture. He also claimed that Jewish immigration had assisted rather than hurt the indigenous Arab population.[16]

Conversely, there was little if any pre-war socialist interest in or links with the Palestinian Arab national movement. Nevertheless, it would be wrong to suggest that all or even most social democrats were sympathetic to Zionism during this period. The movement continued to be divided. Some orthodox socialists including the Austrian socialist leaders Victor Adler and Friedrich Adler, and the ageing Karl Kautsky, continued to portray Zionism as a reactionary movement. The Jewish Labour Bund, which exerted considerable influence within the Socialist International, also remained virulently opposed to Zionism.[17]

From the end of World War Two to the 1967 Six-Day War

Following the events of World War Two including the Holocaust, most of the non-Communist Left wholeheartedly supported the creation of a Jewish national home in Palestine. The Australian Labor Party, as one example, was strongly supportive of the Zionist perspective during 1947–48. Its foreign Minister Dr Herbert Evatt arguably played a key role as Chair of the United Nations Ad Hoc Committee on Palestine in influencing the debate in a pro-partition direction.[18]

The intellectual Left largely followed suit. The French philosopher Jean-Paul Sartre stated in February 1948 that it was 'the duty of non-Jews to help the Jews and the Zionist cause'. Sartre offered unqualified support for Israel during the Arab-Israeli war of the same year and urged the United Nations to provide arms to the Israelis.[19] The prominent left-wing magazine *The Nation* in the United States was also strongly supportive of Israel's creation and, during the key 1947 United Nations debates, sought to expose the alleged earlier pro-Nazi record of leading Palestinian and Arab spokespersons.[20]

More surprising was the Soviet Union's reversal of its traditional anti-Zionist position. The tragedy of the Holocaust appears to have forced some reconsideration of the traditional Marxist belief that the solution to anti-Semitism could only be found via individual assimilation. In May 1947, the Soviet Foreign Minister, Andrei Gromyko, dropped a geo-political bombshell when he expressed support for the partition of Palestine into a Jewish and Arab State. In a passionate speech that broke with traditional communist dogma, Gromyko emphasised the significance of Jewish oppression, the experience of 'almost complete physical annihilation' during the Holocaust, and the continuing plight of the survivors who had lost their homes and livelihood. European culpability, Gromyko argued, lay behind 'the aspiration of the Jews to create their own state. It will be unjust if we ignore this aspiration and deny the Jewish people the right to realize it'. Granted, Gromyko initially expressed a preference for a binational Arab-Jewish State, but added that if 'such a solution proves unworkable because of the deteriorated relations between the Jews and the Arabs, it will be necessary to examine a second solution ... namely, the partition of the country into two independent autonomous states, a Jewish one and an Arab one'.[21]

The Soviet Union and its allies voted in favour of United Nations Resolution 181 (tabled on 29 November 1947) which called for the partition of Palestine into two sovereign states, one Jewish, the other Arab. They then strongly supported the creation of the State of Israel and its war of independence, providing vigorous diplomatic support including a defence of Israel's right to self-defence within United Nations debates, and condemned the 'armed aggression' directed against the Jewish state. They also defended Israel's right to retain strategically significant territory such as the Negev region captured in the 1948 war, and rejected any Israeli responsibility for the Palestinian refugee problem. In addition, the Soviet Union provided via Czechoslovakia badly needed military supplies and the training of pilots and paratroopers which contributed significantly to Israel's military victories in that conflict.[22]

All international Communist parties endorsed the partition plan including those of the Arab world. But after the initial infatuation, the Soviet-Israeli romance quickly cooled. By the early 1950s, the Soviet Union had resumed its traditional hostility to Zionism as reflected in the brutal anti-Zionist show trials of Jewish communists staged by Stalin and his puppet regimes across Eastern Europe, such as the Slánský trial and the Doctors' Plot. Relations deteriorated further in 1955 when the Soviets commenced arms sales to Israel's then sworn enemy, Egypt. They remained hostile until the 1967 Six-Day War as Israel drew closer and closer to the Western powers whilst the Soviets became further entrenched in an alliance with the Arab States.[23] While most Communist parties followed the Soviet line on Israel, they generally did not exhibit the aggressive uniform anti-Zionism that was to become commonplace after the 1967 Six-Day War. Most Communist parties were highly

critical of Israel during that conflict, but nevertheless defended Israel's right to exist. Fidel Castro
reportedly told a European journalist that the
Arabs were wrong to threaten a whole country and
people with extermination.[24]

Social democrats, who had developed their
views in the 1940s in the shadow of Nazism and
the Holocaust, provided considerable political and
ideological support for Israel during this period.[25]
There were various reasons for this sympathy for
Israel. One was the high profile of Israel's collectiv-
ist institutions such as the Histadrut and the kibbutzim, and the domination of Israeli politics by the
social democratic Mapai (Labor) Party. The Socialist International even published an official pamphlet lauding the achievements of Israeli socialism,
including an enthusiastic foreword by the prominent Indian socialist, JB Kripalani.

The pamphlet described the kibbutz as:

an almost perfect microcosm of the Socialist
society – a society of equal and free men
and women who have voluntarily united in a
common effort to realise a new way of social
life; who have abandoned the institutions of
private property and money economy; who
share in their work as they share in the fruits
of their work; and who live according to the
noble Marxian ideal, from each according to his
capacity and to each according to his needs.[26]

The pamphlet also called for immediate Arab recognition of Israel, describing the Middle East dispute as 'fundamentally a conflict between reactionary feudal and semi-fascist autocracies on the one side and a free democracy with unique Socialist achievements on the other'.[27]

A second factor influencing the pro-Israel position was ongoing Western guilt regarding the ineffective response to Nazism and concern about atoning for the Holocaust. A third factor was the reactionary nature of the dictatorial Arab regimes that opposed Israel, which to many people compared unfavourably with Israel's democratic socialist model. There was also no independent Palestinian national movement during this period that sought to claim the attention of socialists to an alternative narrative. Another factor was the prominent involvement of many Jews in Western social democratic parties and broader Left intellectual activity.[28]

Many social democrats and other non-Communist leftists were vocally supportive of Israel in the immediate period prior to and during the 1967 Six-Day War. Martin Luther King and seven other progressive Christian Ministers from the civil rights and anti-war movements signed an open letter to the US President Lyndon Johnson in the *New York Times* in late May. The letter noted that 'Israel is a new nation whose people are still recovering from the horror of the European holocaust', and urged the United States to 'support the independence, integrity and freedom of Israel'.[29] Similarly on

1 June 1967, Sartre and 1500 other left-wing French intellectuals including Simone de Beauvoir, Laurent Schwartz, Pablo Picasso and Claude Lanzmann published a manifesto in *Le Monde* supporting Israel's right to exist as a secure and sovereign state and affirming the sincerity of its quest for peace and dialogue.[30]

The Six-Day War as a turning point

Following the 1967 Six-Day War, a sea change took place in the attitude of the Western Left to Zionism and Israel. Particularly within far Left groups and on university campuses, Israel was increasingly depicted as a modern-day Sparta, allegedly using racist and Nazi-like strategies to suppress Palestinian Arab aspirations in the service of Western imperialism.

The change in Left attitudes can arguably be attributed to five major factors. The first was that the decisive Israeli military victory in the Six-Day War destroyed the post-Holocaust taboo (at least outside the Soviet Union) concerning public criticism of Jews. Jews were suddenly transformed from their historical role as the international symbols of victimhood into an alleged victimiser, whilst the Palestinians became the new symbols of victimhood.[31]

A second factor was the generational change in the Left itself. The older Left (whether orthodox Communist, Trotskyist or social democratic) tended to view the rise of fascism and Nazism and the Holocaust as defining epochs of their political development. Sympathy for the Jews was central to this viewpoint. By contrast, the younger activists involved in the New Left were more influenced by the wrongs of America's intervention in Vietnam. This anti-American animus was rapidly extended to Israel – America's principal ally in the Middle East – which appeared to be the most prominent representative of 'white' Western interests in the Third World.[32]

A third factor influencing the Left's revised position was the significant change in the identity and perception of Israel's enemies. Prior to 1967, it was difficult for any self-respecting group on the Left to back the reactionary monarchs and militarists who opposed Israel's existence. But the war provoked the emergence of an independent Palestinian national movement in the form of the Palestine Liberation Organization (PLO). The PLO began to actively forge links with elements of the Western Left, most particularly the Socialist International, and astutely constructed itself as a key actor in the next stage of the international anti-colonialist struggle.[33]

A fourth factor was the intensive anti-Zionist campaign conducted by the Soviet Union and its sister parties around the world. This campaign introduced many of the key themes that would become dominant within broad sections of the far Left including the equation of Israel and Zionism with apartheid, Nazism and other forms of racism; and arguments that Israel was a uniquely evil state. This campaign buttressed the passage of the November 1975 United Nations General Assembly resolution condemning Zionism as a form of racism.[34] A further factor was that Israel's ongoing occupation of Arab territories, and suppression of Palestinian national aspirations, provoked legitimate criticism from all groups on the Left. This criticism was not identical to the denial of Jewish nationhood and was shared by many Jews and Israelis.

Not all left-wing groups and individuals identified with the anti-Zionist trend. In fact, much of the older Left generation continued to defend Israel's right to exist. This did not mean they were uncritical supporters of Israel. Most rejected the ongoing Israeli occupation of the West Bank and Gaza Strip and urged Israel to recognise Palestinian national rights via a two-state solution. But they emphasised that both Israelis and Palestinians had legitimate national rights and strongly rejected Arab and Palestinian calls for Israel's destruction.[35]

Contemporary Left attitudes

Since 1967, there has continued to be a wide spectrum of Left ideas concerning Zionism and Israel. Equally, attitudes have ebbed and flowed according to events in the Middle East. The mainstream Left became more critical of Israel following the 1982 invasion of Lebanon, and the hardline Israeli government response to the uprising of Palestinians against the occupation known as the First Intifada between 1987 and 1991. But the signing of the Oslo Peace Accord between Israel and the Palestine Liberation Organization in 1993 pushed Left anti-Zionism back to the margins. However, the outbreak of the second Palestinian Intifada in September 2000 and the subsequent Gaza wars between Israel and the Islamic fundamentalist Hamas and also the Lebanese militant Shia grouping Hezbollah, have led to a renewed polarisation of views.

Today, there are arguably three principal Left positions on Zionism and Israel that largely inform progressive attitudes to the BDS movement.

One perspective, which can broadly be called both pro-Israel and pro-Palestinian, is balanced in terms of favouring a two-state solution to facilitate Israeli–Palestinian peace and reconciliation. Advocates support moderates and condemn extremists and violence on both sides of the conflict. This is increasingly a minority position, but is held by a number of centre-left leaders such as the former Australian Labor Party (ALP) Prime Minister Julia Gillard, current ALP Opposition Leader Bill Shorten, the former British New Labour leaders Tony Blair, Gordon Brown and other prominent New Labour figures, and the former German Greens leader and Foreign Minister Joshka Fischer. It is also supported by a number of social democratic and labor party members of parliament in Western countries who have formed Friends of Israel groups, and some prominent social democratic intellectuals.

Other supporters of this perspective include trade unionists around the world, some of whom are represented by the Trade Unions Linking Israel and Palestine (TULIP) group, country-specific trade union Friends of Israel groups, the Geneva Initiative and the wider peace movement in Israel, Left Zionist groups aligned with the Israeli peace movement such as Partners for Progressive Israel, J Street, New Israel Fund Australia, the US-based Third Narrative which was formed by academics to oppose both the West Bank occupation and BDS, and the UK's Engage group, which consists of Jewish and non-Jewish academics opposed to proposals for academic boycotts of Israel.

These groups are unanimously opposed to what they see as the real core aims of the BDS movement, namely to demonise and isolate Israel as a precursor to its destruction. They view the BDS agenda as counterproductive in that it undermines those Israelis most committed to compromise, and discourages the complex Israeli–Palestinian dialogue and negotiations required both on the ground and at government level to progress a peaceful solution.[36] To be sure, some favour a limited boycott of Israeli settlement products, but only in the context of facilitating progress towards a two-state solution based on concessions from both sides of the conflict. A number of these groups have proposed detailed alternative plans for achieving Palestinian national rights.

For example, the long-time Israeli peace activist Hillel Schenker rejects the BDS on three key grounds: it automatically alienates the vast majority of Israelis and Jews worldwide whose support is required to progress a two-state solution because it aims to delegitimise and eliminate the State of Israel; it is widely regarded in the West as having anti-Semitic implications given that it targets all of Israel rather than just the West Bank settlements; and it is an ineffective strategy for progressing Palestinian national rights as governments will not support calls for the elimination of the State of Israel.

Instead, Shenker recommends the following strategies: a constructively critical engagement with the Israeli intellectual and arts communities that endorses activities for peace and reconciliation and conversely attacks government policies that support and expand the West Bank settlements; joint Israeli–Palestinian activities against the occupation via organisations such as the Geneva Initiative and OneVoice; and joint educational work against violence and in favour of conflict resolution.[37]

A second perspective endorses a two-state solution in principle, but in practice holds Israel principally or even solely responsible for the continuing violence and terror in the Middle East. This position, which probably represents the majority of the Western Left, is held by many social democrats, Greens and trade unions, and also by some Jews represented in groups such as the Tikkun community in the United States and the Australian Jewish

Democratic Society. This perspective holds that an end to the Israeli occupation and blockade of the West Bank and Gaza Strip is the key prerequisite for Israeli–Palestinian peace and reconciliation. In general, adherents of this view recognise that not all Israelis are the same, and differentiate between particular Israeli government policies and the Israeli people.

Some components of this second perspective may reasonably be characterised as lacking balance, and fail to offer a corresponding critique of contemporary and historical Palestinian actions and strategies which have acted as serious barriers to peace. Little reference is made to the Palestinian rejection of Israeli offers of statehood at Camp David and Taba in 2000 and 2001, the violence of the Second Intifada, the 2005 election victory of Hamas, and the near-universal Palestinian demand for the return of 1948 refugees to the land within Green Line Israel – the armistice lines of the 1948 Arab-Israeli war.

Many advocates of this perspective present an ambiguous position. They are motivated by a legitimate concern to progress an end to the Israeli occupation of the West Bank, but may be naively drawn into supporting a movement that opposes not the occupation but Israel itself. For example, a number of Greens parties simultaneously state their support for two states, and their support for the BDS movement, even though that movement demands a Greater Palestine.[38] When asked to explain these contradictions, they tend to emphasise their support for a partial BDS, which targets only West Bank settlements and not Green Line Israel. However, the BDS movement has consistently opposed a two-state solution and argued for a boycott of all Israeli Jews.

The third Left perspective is what we term anti-Zionist fundamentalism. This view, which is held mainly but no longer exclusively by far Left groups, regards Israel as a racist, colonialist state which has no right to exist. Adherents hold to a viewpoint opposing Israel's existence specifically and Jewish national rights more broadly which is beyond rational debate and unconnected to contemporary or historical reality. Active support is provided to groups such as Hamas and Hezbollah, which are overtly anti-Jewish as well as anti-Zionist. Suicide bombings and other forms of violence directed against Israeli civilians are viewed as legitimate strategies for eliminating Israel.[39]

This form of anti-Zionism is substantively different to the earlier pre-1948 Left tradition of anti-Zionism. That tradition opposed Zionism as a political movement on theoretical grounds. Anti-Zionist fundamentalists today wish to eliminate the existing nation State of Israel.[40] Israelis and their Jewish supporters are depicted as evil oppressors by way of denying the historical link between the Jewish experience of oppression in *both* Europe and the Middle East and the creation of Israel. Conversely, Palestinians are depicted as intrinsically innocent victims. In place of the objective reality and centrality of the State of Israel to contemporary Jewish identity, anti-Zionist fundamentalists portray Israel as a mere political construct, and utilise ethnic stereotyping of all Israelis and all Jewish supporters of Israel whatever their political views in order to justify their claims.[41]

The purpose of denying the reality of Israel's existence is a ploy to overcome the ideological barrier posed by the Left's historical opposition to racism. Any objective analysis of the Middle East would have to accept that Israel could only be destroyed by a war of partial or total genocide, which would inevitably produce millions of Israeli Jewish refugees. The potential destruction of the world's largest Jewish population just seven decades after the Holocaust would have a catastrophically traumatic effect on almost all of the seven million Jews living outside Israel. But advocacy of genocide means endorsing the most virulent form of racism imaginable. So instead anti-Zionist fundamentalists construct a subjective fantasy world in which Israel is detached from its specifically Jewish roots, and then miraculously destroyed by the political equivalent of a remote control, free of any violence or bloodshed under the banner of anti-racism.[42]

It is this perspective, which seeks to achieve maximalist Palestinian national and human rights at the expense of any national and human rights for Israeli Jews, that drives and informs the core agenda of the BDS movement.

2

The progressive case against Boycott, Divestment and Sanctions

This chapter scrutinises the key arguments and strategies of the BDS movement. We start with a chronological overview of the major BDS activities from 2001 to 2014 followed by an examination of their three key aims pertaining to the Palestinian Right of Return, equality for Palestinians inside Green Line Israel and an end to the West Bank occupation. We also dissect the crude allegation that Israel is an apartheid state.

The chapter then proceeds to reveal the fundamentalist agenda of BDS. We begin by exposing the differences between the BDS campaign and the more moderate perspective of the modern-day Palestinian Authority, and illustrate the historical links between the BDS's one-state agenda and the earlier campaigns of the PLO and Arab world for the destruction of Israel. We also document the movement's bitter attacks on two-state advocates, its frequent use of anti-Semitism or contempt for the victims of anti-Semitism, its targeting of Israeli and Jewish individuals using McCarthyist-style attacks, and its opportunistic exploitation of Jewish anti-Zionists. Additionally, we argue that the movement mainly serves to strengthen the Israeli political Right and does little to progress Palestinian national or human rights.

The chronology of the BDS

The BDS movement emerged as a by-product of the outbreak of the second Palestinian Intifada in September 2000 and the associated collapse of the Oslo Peace Accord based on the concept of peaceful negotiations and mutual compromise. The glimmer of hope offered up by the mid-to-late 1990s peace process has given way to the renewed polarisation of the Israeli and Palestinian peoples and their narratives.

The BDS represents a return to the earlier pre-1993 Palestinian viewpoint that Israel is not a legitimate state, that Palestinian aspirations can be advanced only via zero-sum conflict at the expense of Israel, and that all possible forms of pressure should be used to coerce Israel into surrendering to Palestinian demands. It also reflects an understanding that the violent strategies such as suicide bombings and rocket attacks that characterised the Second Intifada have failed (at least in Western eyes). However, it is in essence a continuation of the Palestinian war against Israel by non-violent means.

The specific catalyst for the BDS movement was the World Conference against Racism, Racial Discrimination, Xenophobia and Related Intolerance (WCAR) held in Durban, South Africa in September 2001. It was the Non-Governmental Organisations (NGO) forum at this conference who launched a campaign to demonise and isolate Israel. Nine official declarations relating to the Israeli–Palestinian conflict were passed by the forum, dwarfing the attention paid to other ethnic and religious conflicts. Article 419 provocatively called for the 'reinstitution of UN resolution 3379 [first passed in the 1970s] determining the practices of Zionism as racist' because it allegedly 'propagate[d] the racial domination of one group over another through the implementation of all measures designed to drive out other indigenous groups'. Elsewhere two articles made the case for instituting an organised campaign against Israel. Article 425 called for the international community to work towards the 'complete and total isolation of Israel' through 'mandatory and comprehensive sanctions and embargoes' as well as the 'full cessation of all links (diplomatic, economic, social, aid, military co-operation) between all states and Israel'. Article 425 anticipated the formal BDS campaign that followed. The aims of the campaign to isolate Israel were to be achieved through an 'international anti Israeli [sic] Apartheid movement as implemented against South African Apartheid through a global solidarity campaign network of international civil society, UN bodies and agencies, business communities and to end the conspiracy of silence among states, particularly the European Union and the United States.'[1]

The Declaration was accompanied by the widespread distribution of literature that was overtly anti-Jewish as well as anti-Zionist. Up to 20 000 flyers were issued by the Islamic Propagation Centre, spruiking the 'good things' that would have resulted had Nazi Germany won World War Two, implicitly suggesting that Israel would not have been created. Copies of the Tsarist-era, anti-Semitic Protocols of the Elders of Zion – a document known to be fraudulent – were also widely circulated.[2] Representatives from the United States, Australia, Canada and other countries walked out of the forum in disgust.

The Durban Declaration underpinned the international campaign for an academic boycott of Israel, which was publicly launched by British academics Steven and Hilary Rose in April 2002.[3] The timing of the launch was instructive. It commenced immediately after the height of the Palestinian suicide bombing attacks in March 2002, which killed 63 Israelis and injured many hundreds. These attacks, which culminated in the attack on the Passover Seder in Netanya's Park Hotel that killed 30 people and injured 140, provoked the Israeli invasion of the leading West Bank cities in an attempt to destroy the terror networks and stop the carnage.

In chapter 4 we specifically examine the actions of British academic activists and the resultant debate within the academy and elsewhere.

Notably most of these early boycott actions were undertaken by international actors rather than by the Palestinians themselves. The first Palestinian initiative seems to date to July 2004 when 60 Palestinian academic and other non-government organisations publicly called for an academic and cultural boycott of Israel. The statement claimed that:

> The Israeli academy has contributed, either directly or indirectly, to maintaining, defending or otherwise justifying the military occupation and colonization of the West Bank and Gaza; the entrenched system of racial discrimination and segregation against the Palestinian citizens of Israel, which resembles the defunct apartheid system in South Africa; and the denial of the fundamental rights of Palestinian refugees in contravention of international law.[4]

An updated version of this Palestinian call for a general Boycott, Divestment and Sanctions campaign against Israel was issued by 170 Palestinian organisations in July 2005.[5] Any pretence of excusing the 'good' Israeli was dispensed with when a revised set of boycott guidelines issued by PACBI in July 2014 urged a blanket boycott, alleging Israeli academia to be 'profoundly implicated in supporting and perpetuating Israel's systematic denial of Palestinian rights'.[6] The guidelines preclude any collaboration between Palestinian-Arab and Israeli academics other than activities that specifically endorse a hard-line Palestinian narrative aimed at undermining the very existence of Israel. In short, the boycott seeks to prevent any Israeli–Palestinian reconciliation and conflict resolution.[7]

The Palestinian call seems to have been influential in provoking action by the two British academic unions, the Association of University Teachers (AUT) and the National Association of Teachers in Further and Higher Education (NATFHE), which later merged in 2006 to form the University and College Union (UCU). We further examine these controversial events in chapter 4, as well as other major international manifestations of the BDS movement that include the following:

- boycott motions and campaigns by trade unions in England, Ireland, Canada, South Africa, Australia, the USA and Europe
- cultural boycotts by some leading scientists, authors, artists, filmmakers, actors, musicians and performers including Roger Waters, Carlos Santana, Elvis Costello, Naomi Klein, Emma Thompson and Stephen Hawking
- boycott initiatives in the form of divestment by churches including the World Council of Churches and the Presbyterian Church USA
- a decision by the University of Johannesburg in South Africa to end links with Ben-Gurion

University in Israel
- moves by some European banks and investment funds to desist from involvement with Israeli banks or investments[8]
- the apparent infiltration by the BDS movement of American academia, evidenced by a number of bodies recently passing boycott motions.[9]

In 2014, prior to the onset of the July–August war between Israel and Hamas forces based in Gaza, the American Secretary of State John Kerry warned that the BDS movement might gain greater support if current peace negotiations do not succeed.[10]

So has the BDS movement been a success or failure? On the one hand, it appears to have had some adverse effect on Israeli academic and cultural life, and contributed to some isolation from the international community. On the other hand, it appears to have had limited economic and political impact. The high-tech, export-oriented Israeli economy, worth US$305 billion according to the International Monetary Fund, is currently growing and attracting significant international investment.[11] And no Western countries have broken off diplomatic relations, nor are likely to do so. So the BDS movement, whilst enjoying some micro-victories, has definitely not achieved its core objectives. But a BDS that produced a serious economic and political boycott against Israel could prove another matter. In early 2014, the then Israeli Finance Minister Yair Lapid expressed a fear that if significant

European economic sanctions (such as ending the supply of European Union (EU) funding for joint Israeli-European projects and prohibitions on investing in particular Israeli-owned enterprises) were introduced they could cost 10 000 Israeli jobs, cause a rupture of trade with the EU, presently a third of Israel's total, to fall by $5.7 billion, and produce a massive increase in the price of consumer goods and the cost of living.[12]

The three key aims of the BDS movement

To examine why BDS has achieved limited success it is necessary to explore its stated aims. Both the July 2004 and July 2005 statements by the Palestinian Campaign for the Academic and Cultural Boycott of Israel (PACBI) emphasise three key aims:

- to end the Israeli occupation of lands occupied in the 1967 war including East Jerusalem, and dismantle the security barrier
- to achieve full equality for the Arab-Palestinian citizens of Israel
- to support the rights of Palestinian refugees including their demand for a Right of Return to Israel as implied by UN Resolution 194.[13]

We consider each of these aims in turn, and particularly whether or not they are compatible with a two-state solution and mainstream political support.

Firstly, the call for an end to the Israeli military occupation of the West Bank including East Jerusalem, Gaza Strip and the Syrian Golan Heights seems on the surface to be a reasonable demand, and potentially compatible with a two-state perspective. However, the language used in the PACBI documents is open to some ambiguous interpretations.[14] The 2005 statement demands that Israel 'end its occupation and colonization of all Arab lands'. Given that the Palestinian national movement prior to 1993 defined even Israel within the Green Line borders as Occupied Palestine, this could mean a rejection of Israel's very existence. It is also surprising that the statement refers to the Golan Heights given that this is presumably a matter for negotiation between Israel and Syria, with no direct link to the Palestinians.

In fact, key BDS leaders suggest that the meaning of occupied territory is intended to denote Green Line Israel. 'If the Occupation ends, would that end our call for BDS?' Omar Barghouti, a Qatari-born leader of the BDS campaign and, ironically, a PhD student based at Tel Aviv University, asked in 2010. 'No, it wouldn't'. In response to another interview conducted in the same year he asserted. 'If the refugees were to return, you would not have a two-state solution. You would have a Palestine next to a Palestine, rather than a Palestine next to Israel.'[15]

Another concern is that the statement ignores any genuine Israeli concerns about potential military threats following an Israeli withdrawal from the

West Bank. The reality is that following the removal of troops and settlers from the Gaza Strip in 2005 Israel was inundated with rockets fired from the evacuated territory. Israel is not likely to allow a similar situation to occur in the West Bank given that the firing of rockets or missiles from the geographically high territory onto the heavily populated Israeli coastal plains below could suffocate the life of the country.[16] Related to this aim is the demand to dismantle the West Bank security barrier. Undeniably, the barrier has stopped the suicide bombings and terror attacks launched against Israel. In the absence of a negotiated final status agreement, dismantling of the barrier is simply not going to transpire. In short, any arrangement to end the occupation will need to respect the security needs of Israel as well as the right of the Palestinians to national independence. Otherwise an Israeli withdrawal may lead to only greater violence, as happened in the case of Gaza.

Secondly, the call for equality for Arabs living in Israel also seems potentially in accord with a two-state solution. Yet the ambiguous language used in the BDS statements suggests that the true agenda may not be civil equality for all citizens of Israel, but rather collective national rights for Arabs requiring the transformation of Israel into a binational state, or worse. As such, BDS supporters are prone to suggest that Jews are not a bona fide nation deserving of national rights of their own. Rather, they are a religious minority to be tolerated by the Arab world.

Some advocates are quite explicit on this point. As Mustafa Barghouti, Palestinian politician and activist, wrote in 2012: 'Irrespective of what political settlement is ultimately embraced, Palestinians need a unified strategy for overcoming Israeli racism, apartheid and oppression'. In his opinion, what is ultimately required however is a 'single democratic state (not the single binational state) in which all citizens have equal rights and duties regardless of their religious affiliation and origins'. To his mind, this was the only 'alternative to the attempt to force Palestinians to accept slavery under occupation and an apartheid order in the form of a feeble autonomous government that is dubbed a state'.[17]

Arab Israelis constitute about 20 per cent of the population or 1.7 million people. In principle, Arab citizens enjoy formal equality including freedom of speech, assembly and movement, the right to vote and equal access to health care, education and employment. There are 12 Arab Members of the Israeli Knesset (out of 120) who vocally critique Israeli policies. Arabs have served as members of Cabinet, in prominent positions in the civil service and hospitals, as judges and diplomats and in senior positions in the police and army. Arabic is officially recognised as Israel's second language.[18]

To be sure, even supporters of Israel acknowledge that Arabs experience systemic disadvantage including disproportionate poverty, under-funding of housing and infrastructure, low representation in professional employment, higher death rates from preventable diseases, much lower participation rates in higher education and limited resources allocated to Arab schools. But they argue that Israel is actively working to reduce inequalities experienced by the Arab minority citing initiatives to promote Arab employment and economic development, increase recruitment to the civil service, equalise access to welfare payments and facilitate greater access to higher education.[19]

Critics of Israel, in contrast, argue that Israel's self-definition as a Jewish state creates inherent discrimination towards its non-Jewish citizens. They often refer to the Law of Return, which privileges citizenship rights for Jews from all over the globe. Associated concerns relate to the Jewishness of the national flag, anthem and associated national symbols, land laws which privilege Jewish ownership and the state's refusal to recognise or provide services to many Arab villages.[20]

A recent text by two US specialists in Israeli studies arguably provides a balanced analysis. They argue that Arabs are second-class citizens in Israel given ongoing socio-economic disadvantage and exclusion as evidenced in high rates of poverty and unemployment, low income levels, limited occupational opportunities and lack of access to land. But nevertheless they do not support Palestinian demands for Israel to abandon its Jewish identity and become a binational state. Rather, they propose a series of practical measures within Israel to address the manifestations of inequality and discrimination including recognising the Palestinians as a national minority group, facilitating increased cultural autonomy, introducing laws to protect Arabs from official or popular prejudice and establishing affirmative action programs to enhance their socio-economic status.[21] These measures appear to address the concerns raised by the BDS movement regarding equal citizenship while remaining congruent with a two-state solution.

The third and most controversial demand is for a Palestinian Right of Return. This aim is highlighted in the 2004 PACBI statement and it underlines how the BDS campaign remains at best ambivalent about a two-state solution. The statement emphasises that the first and foremost priority of BDS is to reverse the events of 1948 – the foundation of Israel – that led to the Palestinian refugee tragedy (generally referred to as the Nakba, or 'catastrophe', to describe the expulsion or voluntary departure of Palestinian Arabs from their homes during the 1948 Arab-Israeli war) and, secondly, to demand the unconditional return of the 1948 Palestinian refugees and their millions of descendants to their former homes inside Green Line Israel.

The inclusion of the Right of Return is no aberration. Indeed, many key BDS activists, such as Omar Barghouti, along with the Jewish-Australian journalist Antony Loewenstein, call for the establishment of a 'secular democratic state' of Palestine. This is the so-called one-state solution, which would see a single, non-Jewish state magically created between the Jordan River and the Mediterranean Sea, ushering in the end of the State of Israel after 66 years in existence. Thus, BDS is justly regarded by many as a war against Israel by means other than war. '[T]he inability to wage [conventional] war', argued Mustafa Barghouti in 2012, 'does not automatically mean we have to surrender and eschew other means of struggle'.[22]

The mass return of potentially six million Palestinians living in refugee camps and the diaspora would change the demographic composition of Israel profoundly and almost certainly turn the Jewish population into a disempowered minority. It is inherently inconsistent with a two-state solution. Even prominent anti-Zionist Noam Chomsky has described the inclusion of this demand as enjoying little international support, lacking any basis in international law and 'virtually guaranteeing the failure' of the BDS campaign.[23]

The concept of a Palestinian Right of Return is based on the United Nations General Assembly Resolution 194 of December 1948. The Resolution stated that:

> the refugees wishing to return to their homes
> and live at peace with their neighbors should
> be permitted to do so at the earliest practicable
> date, and that compensation should be paid for
> the property of those choosing not to return
> and for loss of or damage to property which,
> under principles of international law or equity,

should be made good by the governments or authorities responsible'.[24]

The meaning of this resolution was clearly conditional, and its implementation dependent on conflict resolution and Israeli–Palestinian reconciliation.[25] It was formally linked to acceptance of the earlier UN partition resolution creating both Jewish and Arab states in Palestine, and a negotiated peace. In practice, both the Palestinian leaders and the Arab governments initially rejected the resolution precisely because it implied recognition of Israel's legitimacy.[26]

Prior to the 1967 Six-Day War, Palestinian Right of Return rhetoric was used to deny the legitimacy of the State of Israel, and so provide a rationale for the Arab refusal to recognise the State of Israel. However, following the 1967 war, the international debate shifted from questions about the legitimacy of Israel within the Green Line borders to questions about the legitimacy of a Palestinian State in the West Bank or Gaza Strip. The subsequent political contest for or against a two-state solution explicitly assumed that any resolution of the Palestinian refugee tragedy would be addressed within the territories occupied by Israel in 1967. There could be two states or there could be a Palestinian Right of Return, but there could not be both. It was instructive that the Oslo Peace Accord signed by Israel and the PLO in 1993 did not mention Resolution 194.[27]

Given the current hatred between Israelis and Palestinians it is very likely that any large-scale return of 1948 Palestinian refugees to Israel would bring civil war and enormous bloodshed rather than Israeli–Palestinian peace and reconciliation. The only sane and dignified solution to the refugee tragedy is the resettlement of all Palestinian refugees with compensation as either full citizens in the neighboring Arab countries in which most have lived for over 65 years, or alternatively as citizens of a new Palestinian state to be established alongside Israel in the West Bank and Gaza Strip. Yet such a resolution to the Palestinian refugee tragedy is anathema to BDS activists.

The BDS and 'Israeli apartheid'

Accompanying the three key aims of the BDS campaign is the associated allegation that Israel is an apartheid state similar to what existed in South Africa. This accusation is intended to turn Israel into a pariah state, and so justify the application of the same boycott measures that were originally used against the apartheid regime of South Africa.[28] Hence it is not surprising that the 2004 PACBI statement makes three separate references to Israel's alleged 'system of apartheid'.[29] It remains a staple of BDS propaganda.

However, the Israel–apartheid analogy is seriously flawed on historical, political and factual grounds. The historical basis of this analogy is the anti-Zionist campaign launched by the Soviet Union following the 1967 Six-Day War. This campaign, which quickly transgressed into overt anti-Semitism, advanced allegations that Zionism was a tool of Western imperialism including Jewish capitalism, Zionists had collaborated with the Nazis to perpetrate the Holocaust, Zionism exerted disproportionate power and influence throughout the capitalist world, and Zionism was a racist philosophy similar to Nazism. The equation of Israel with apartheid South Africa was central to this ongoing campaign, which peaked with the United Nations adoption of the 'Zionism is racism' resolution in 1975 (later to be rescinded in 1991). It was this analogy, based on an anti-Semitic conspiracy worldview, which was revived at the previously discussed Durban conference.[30]

Factually there is little if any resemblance between Israel and South Africa. South Africa was a racist state based on a small white minority oppressing a large black majority. In contrast, the Israeli–Palestinian conflict is not race-based, but rather a clash between two legitimate competing nationalisms.[31] Notably, key BDS campaigners such as Omar Barghouti simplistically construct all Israeli Jews as 'white Europeans' who originate from Poland vis-à-vis brown-skinned Palestinians.[32] But in fact many Israeli Jews (both the large number of Mizrahim from Arab or North African backgrounds comprising about 50 per cent of the Jewish population, and the black Falasha community from Ethiopia) are just as dark-skinned as their Palestinian Arab neighbours.

From the late 1940s, South Africa introduced institutional discrimination, which segregated the white and black communities. Blacks were excluded from voting, restricted from living or working or using public facilities in specific areas and forbidden to engage in sexual or marital relations with whites. In contrast, Arabs enjoy formal equality in Israel and significant political, social and cultural freedoms.[33] This is not to deny, as noted above, that official and popular discrimination exists. But this discrimination is arguably no different to that experienced by various religious minorities in Arab countries – such as the Christian Copts in Egypt – by black people in the United States, and by ethnic and religious minorities such as Arabs or Muslims in significant parts of Europe.[34]

To be sure, the experience of Arab citizens of Israel is qualitatively different to that of Palestinians living under military occupation in the West Bank. The latter are subject to oppression of their national and human rights sometimes due to military or security concerns, and sometimes solely as a result of nationalist ideological agendas driven by the Israeli Government or the settler movement.[35] But this oppression is not race-based.

The apartheid analogy is not only false but politically counterproductive. The Israelis are depicted as inherently evil oppressors who deserve to be demonised, and the Palestinians as defenceless and innocent victims who are infantilised. This simplistic construction only encourages the Palestinians to dream of ending Israel's existence. It is the precise opposite of the difficult negotiations involving mutual concessions and compromise required to advance peace and reconciliation.[36]

The BDS and one state or two states

It should be evident from the earlier discussion of BDS aims that the movement does not favour a two-state solution to the Israeli–Palestinian conflict. Rather, the movement demands the return of millions of Palestinian refugees to Green Line Israel, which will mean transforming Israel into an Arab majority state of Greater Palestine.[37]

The key leaders of the BDS movement such as Omar Barghouti and Ali Abunimah, the American-born and -based Palestinian activist and co-founder of *The Electronic Intifada* website, openly state their preference for the so-called one-state solution. Barghouti admits that 'for more than 28 years, I have, in my personal capacity, consistently and openly advocated a secular democratic state in the entire area of historic Palestine, where everyone enjoys equal rights, irrespective of ethnicity, religion or any identity attribute'.[38] He emphasises that this does not mean a binational state in which Israeli Jews would share national sovereignty with

Palestinian Arabs because he does not believe the Jews deserve national rights. Rather, he proposes an Arab-dominated Greater Palestine populated by millions of returning Palestinian refugees in which Jews would be permitted to remain as a tolerated religious minority. He also concedes that a Palestinian Right of Return cannot possibly be reconciled with a two-state solution.[39]

Barghouti's proposal represents a strange regression to the PLO's 1969 call via the Palestine Covenant for a secular, democratic state of Palestine. The PLO always clarified that this did not mean a binational Palestine in which Israeli Jews and Palestinian Arabs would live as equals. Rather, Palestine would be an exclusively Arab state in which the Jews (or some Jews) would enjoy cultural and religious freedom, but no national rights.[40]

Abunimah states that Israel should be replaced by a single state for two peoples although to his partial credit he at least implies this would be a binational state that recognised the national rights of both peoples.[41] Albeit in a later statement he cautions that Israeli Jews should only enjoy rights as individual citizens, not as members of 'a distinct national group'.[42] Other leading BDS campaigners also propose an end to Israel's existence. Noura Erakat, the Palestinian-American academic and BDS activist, favours a single state that allocates citizenship rights based on religion, a recipe for trouble.[43]

Bill Mullen, a leader of the US Campaign for the Academic and Cultural Boycott of Israel

(USACBI), depicts Israel as an illegitimate state founded by ethnic cleansing.[44] Another prominent BDS activist, Anna Baltzer, the National Organizer of the US campaign to end the Israeli occupation, favours a one-state solution, which she suggests would involve 'equal rights for all' in a 'binational secular state'.[45] So too does Josh Ruebner, the National Advocacy Director of the US Campaign to End the Israeli Occupation, as does David Lloyd, a founding member of USACBI.[46]

The pro-BDS American Studies Association opposes the very existence of Israel, rather than just the Israeli occupation of the West Bank.[47] Similarly, Australians for Palestine reject a partial boycott aimed only at West Bank settlement goods in that 'such boycotts fail to target the repressive state itself which is instrumental in the colonial expansion of Palestinian lands through the settlement project'.[48] Leading figures in the UK academic boycott movement such as Sue Blackwell and Steve Cushion as well as George Galloway have also demanded Israel's destruction.[49]

Yet oddly, members of the BDS movement continually state that they have no position for or against two states versus one state,[50] which suggests that they have no position for or against the national rights of Israel's six million Jews. It is obvious that this non-adoption of a position is disingenuous given that as noted above most of the leading BDS spokespersons such as Barghouti and Abuminah personally support one state, and no prominent

BDS leaders have actively argued in favour of two states.

Even long-time supporters of the Palestinians such as Norman Finkelstein have criticised this charade. Finkelstein argued that BDS campaigners were dishonest and the equivalent of a religious 'cult' because they refused to admit that their real goal was to destroy Israel. He stated:

> I loathe the disingenuous. They don't want
> Israel. They think they are being very clever.
> They call it their three tier. We want the end
> of the occupation, the Right of Return, and we
> want equal rights for Arabs in Israel. And they
> think they are very clever because they know the
> result of implementing all three is what, what is
> the result? You know and I know what the result
> is. There's no Israel.

Instead, Finkelstein has urged BDS campaigners to end their 'duplicity', eschew the extreme one-state agenda, recognise Israel and support a two-state solution.[51]

But the BDS movement's refusal to adopt a clear perspective on conflict resolution arguably reflects a range of complex pragmatic concerns and agendas including foremost a concern to unify rather than split the movement. Firstly, the Palestinian Authority clearly supports two states and the BDS movement does not want to alienate this body, which is still recognised by the international community as the official representative of the Palestinian people. The Palestinian Authority President Mahmoud Abbas has stated unequivocally:

> No we do not support the boycott of Israel.
> But we ask everyone to boycott the products
> of the settlements. Because the settlements
> are in our territories. It is illegal ... But we
> don't ask anyone to boycott Israel itself. We
> have relations with Israel, we have mutual
> recognition of Israel.[52]

Similarly, the Palestinian General Federation of Trade Unions (PGFTU) has rejected proposals by Western trade unions to break links with the Histadrut. Instead, they have urged the maintenance of links as a means of actively pressuring the Histadrut to oppose the occupation and support two states. Nasser Younis, the leader of the Palestinian General Union for Transport Workers, even cosponsored a motion at the 2010 meeting of the International Transport Workers Federation praising Israeli–Palestinian trade union co-operation and urging a two-state solution.[53]

Neither the Palestinian Authority nor the Palestinian General Federation of Trade Unions supports a blanket BDS. Additionally, a minority of Palestinian academics including Sari Nusseibeh, the President of Al-Quds University in East Jerusalem, oppose academic boycotts of Israel. Nusseibeh has argued that academic co-operation is essential to facilitate peaceful dialogue and conflict resolution between the two peoples.[54] Similarly, Palestinian journalist and academic Daoud Kuttab has warned that 'by boycotting Israelis one tends to lump the entire population into one basket, including those who are publicly supportive of Palestinians'.[55]

Secondly, most of the small number of Jews and even smaller number of Israelis who support a BDS (even in most cases a targeted form of BDS that applies only to the West Bank settlements) also favour a two-state solution. Additionally, the international community, including many pro-Palestinians, also supports two states.

Conversely, the strongest Palestinian supporter of the one-state solution is Hamas, which demands the violent destruction of the State of Israel. It cannot be denied that Hamas and the BDS movement share the same goal of eliminating the State of Israel even if their proposed strategies differ.[56] But the BDS movement does not want to be associated politically with Hamas both because Hamas is persona non grata with most of the international community, and also because many leading BDS activists identify as secular liberals, rather than as far-right religious fundamentalists.

The BDS movement vilifies supporters of two states

Much of the BDS movement's anger is directed not at Israeli and Jewish hawks who deny the legitimacy of Palestinian aspirations, but rather at left-wing Jews and others who support a two-state solution that recognises both Israeli and Palestinian national rights.

The PACBI has consistently opposed strategies to progress Israeli–Palestinian peace and reconciliation. A major initiative by the One Voice organisation to hold simultaneous concerts in Tel Aviv, Jericho and other cities to promote a negotiated two-state solution was opposed by the PACBI. Instead, they urged Palestinians to boycott the Jericho concert, which was later cancelled due to threats of violence.[57] BDS leader Omar Barghouti has slammed the Israeli Left for rejecting only the occupation, rather than the very existence of Israel. He accuses prominent peace activists such as Amos Oz and Uri Avnery of being 'racists' because they refuse to support the extreme demands of the BDS movement for an unlimited Palestinian Right of Return.[58]

A similar targeting of supporters of mutual compromise has occurred elsewhere. Professor Mona Baker of the University of Manchester specifically sacked two left-wing Israelis from the Editorial Boards of her journals, as we will examine in chapter 4. The radical left-wing Israeli academic Oren Yiftachel, who labels Israel an 'ethnocracy' rather than a democracy, found his articles excluded from the journal *Political Geography*.[59]

The leading Irish BDS activist David Landy aggressively castigates the Israeli Peace Now movement and similar groups internationally for allegedly supporting Israeli military actions against the Palestinians, and opposing instead of collaborating with hardline pro-Palestinian lobbyists.[60] The American BDS activist Donna Nevel has sharply rebuked the left-wing J Street organisation for opposing the BDS movement,[61] and the Palestinian-American BDS activist Noura Erakat bitterly attacks what she calls 'liberal Zionists' who question the targeting of Israel as a whole, rather than just the West Bank occupation.[62]

In Australia, academic and BDS activist Ned Curthoys similarly targeted his principal attack not on conservative supporters of Israel, but rather on so-called 'Left-Zionists' who are active in other left-wing causes and support Palestinian national rights, but also defend Israel's right to exist.[63] So did BDS activist Samah Sabawi who furiously attacked Israeli peace activist and New Israel Fund President Naomi Chazan's opposition to the elimination of the State of Israel.[64] And Australians for Palestine attacked the Trade Unions Linking Israel and Palestine (TULIP) group for favouring dialogue between Israel and Palestinian trade unions leading to a two-state solution.[65]

The historical context of movements boycotting Jews and Israel

The BDS campaign is merely the latest in a long history of campaigns to boycott and isolate Jews and Israel. The best known was the boycott of Jewish businesses by the Nazi regime in Germany. The Nazis also expelled all Jewish academics from the universities, publicly burnt books by Jewish authors and excluded Jews from the professions and public and cultural institutions.[66]

The longest-running boycott has been the Arab League campaign formed in 1945 to ban Jewish products and manufactured goods from Palestine and, since 1948, a boycott against the State of Israel. The boycott campaign has three tiers. The primary boycott precludes Arab League members from trading with either the Israeli Government or an Israeli citizen. The secondary boycott extends the ban to any global firms that conduct business with Israel. The tertiary boycott proscribes commercial relationships with companies that do business with other firms that have been blacklisted by the Arab League.

The boycott is no longer observed by all Arab countries and may have only minimal impact on the Israeli economy. Egypt, Jordan and the Palestinian Authority, for example, have signed peace treaties with Israel and engage in limited trade with Israel. It seems, however, that the boycott retains at least some 'symbolic importance' for those Arabs who oppose any normalisation of relations with Israel.[67]

Two leading Canadian BDS advocates, Abigail Bakan and Yameen Abu-Laban, are critical of the Arab League boycott, which they believe has been ineffective in advancing the Palestinian struggle against Israel. They compare the Arab League campaign unfavourably with the BDS on the grounds that the former involves states rather than popular action by peoples, and is only regional rather than international in its membership and application.[68] But they arguably miss the key common feature of the Arab League boycott and the BDS movement, which is that both campaigns seek to stereotype and ostracise all Israeli Jews as the national and political enemy.

Another historical manifestation of 'anti-Zionist' boycotts was the disaffiliation by some UK student unions of Jewish student societies from 1977 until the mid-1980s on the spurious grounds that they were Zionist and hence allegedly racist.[69] These actions were driven by the far-left British Anti-Zionist Organisation, which used openly anti-Semitic arguments comparing Israel to Nazi Germany, and led to a number of examples of overt discrimination against Jewish students, which left-wing writer Christopher Hitchens, channelling the German socialist politician August Bebel, aptly called 'the socialism of fools'.[70]

The BDS movement
promotes hate speech

The international BDS movement has always targeted not only the Jewish population of the State of Israel, but additionally all Jews worldwide who support the continued existence of Israel whatever their political views on conflict resolution, as the political enemy. Yet the movement is highly sensitive to charges of anti-Semitism.

The Palestinian BDS National Committee vehemently denied what they called 'inflammatory accusations of anti-Semitism' pertaining to the pro-BDS motion passed by Marrickville Council in Australia. They alleged that these allegations were 'patently false, intellectually and morally dishonest, and serve to discredit and silence any form of criticism directed against Israel's war crimes and human rights abuses'.[71]

Prominent Australian BDS advocates including academics Stuart Rees and Peter Slezak, independent journalist Antony Loewenstein, far-left activist Kim Bullimore and lawyer and author Randa Abdel-Fattah have also denied that there is any anti-Semitic agenda behind the BDS movement.[72] Loewenstein has dismissed accusations of anti-Semitism as an allegedly disingenuous attempt by Zionist groups to restrict debate on Middle East policy. He argues that what he calls a 'crying wolf syndrome' has made it harder to take action against what he contrasts as 'real anti-Semitism'.[73]

Similarly, the Irish BDS activist John Landy both dismisses allegations of anti-Semitism as a trivial matter, and also suggests that they are used cynically by the Zionist movement to unite Jews behind Israel and discredit opponents.[74] An American BDS activist has even suggested that aligning anti-Semitism with anti-Zionism 'alters the fundamental meaning of anti-Semitism from something noxious to something honorable'.[75]

These arguments suggest erroneously that anti-Zionism and anti-Semitism never converge, that there is no difference between reasonable criticism of Israeli policies and the demonisation and ethnic stereotyping of Israel and all Israeli Jews, and that accusations of anti-Semitism are levelled dishonestly and in bad faith by pro-Israel lobbyists who wish to prevent any criticisms of Israel. The UK scholar David Hirsh has called this tactic the Livingstone formulation named after the Mayor of London, Ken Livingstone, who attempted to deflect justified accusations of anti-Semitism by claiming without any relevant connection to his own actions that critics were motivated by a concern to stifle criticism of Israel.[76]

Such arguments also ignore the fact that it is generally victims of racism who are given the right to define the meaning and content of racism, not those who may be aiding and abetting such ethnocentric prejudices. The famous Macpherson Report into the racist murder of a black teenager in London in 1993 is a useful example. It established that racism involves 'any incident which is perceived to be racist by the victim or any other person'.[77] Consequently, it is the Jewish community that is best able to judge whether attacks on the State of Israel rather than specific Israeli policies may constitute anti-Semitism.[78]

Even if Loewenstein and other BDS advocates were principled opponents of anti-Semitism, the problem remains that their statements against anti-Semitism are too often contradicted by the actions of the BDS movement. This has been particularly evident in the United Kingdom where the University and College Union has been at the forefront of pro-BDS activities, and was widely accused by members and commentators of promoting an institutional culture of anti-Semitism.

The UCU rejected and denounced the frequently utilised and balanced European Monitoring Centre on Racism and Xenophobia (EUMC) working definition of anti-Semitism – which carefully distinguished between criticisms of Israeli policies similar to those of other countries and fanatical anti-Zionism, which employed traditional anti-Jewish stereotypes – on the grounds that criticism of Israel cannot possibly be anti-Semitic. This is patently absurd given that many fanatical anti-Zionists come not only from the supposedly anti-racist far Left, but also from the openly racist far Right (such as the American neo-Nazi David Duke).[79]

As chapter 4 reveals, UCU debates over implementing a boycott of Israeli universities have been frequently occasioned by manifestations of anti-Semitism ranging from allegations of Zionist political and financial control to the distribution of far-right propaganda.

One of the most shocking examples of BDS activism exhibiting an anti-Semitic character occurred in South Africa during 2013. *Dubula e Juda*, which means 'shoot the Jew', a spin on the controversial black South African struggle song, *Dubula ibhunu* (calling for Boers to be shot), was sung by BDS supporters outside Wits University's Great Hall. Muhammed Desai, co-ordinator of BDS South Africa, sought to explain the song's use: 'Just like you would say "kill the Boer" at a funeral during the eighties; it wasn't about killing white people, it was used as a way of identifying with the apartheid regime.' 'The whole idea of anti-Semitism is blown out of proportion', he insisted. After a public outcry, BDS South Africa eventually offered a muted apology in the process attacking Zionism as a form of 'racism'.[80] In early 2014, an article entitled 'The Jewish hand behind Internet, Google, Facebook, Wikipedia, Yahoo!, MySpace, eBay', published on the website of a prominent Dutch BDS spokesperson Gretta Duisenberg (www.stopdebezetting.com –'stop the occupation') was the subject of a criminal complaint by two anti-racist organisations.[81]

There have also been a number of examples of overt anti-Semitism emanating from the BDS movement in Australia. In one instance, aggressive anti-Jewish messages were posted in a Facebook page established to support protests against a Max Brenner chocolate store at the University of New South Wales. These included allegations that Jews were an evil money-hungry people who controlled the media, and suggestions that the Holocaust was invented by Zionists to support the establishment of Israel.[82]

Other Australian BDS advocates have employed old-fashioned racist motifs accusing Jews of wielding disproportionate power and influence over the media and politicians. One such advocate, journalist Antony Loewenstein, alleged a conspiracy of 'Zionist lobbying and money' connected with sympathisers with Jewish-sounding names in the Australian Workers' Union (AWU) to influence Australia's Middle East policy.[83] Loewenstein was later forced to apologise for naming AWU health and safety expert Dr Yossi Berger as a 'Zionist advocate' even though Berger has never publicly expressed any viewpoint on Israel. He later also admitted that the union's national secretary Paul Howes, whom he alleged was the beneficiary of a paid propaganda trip to Israel by Australian-based Zionist lobbyists, had never visited the country.[84]

Elsewhere, Loewenstein referred to the alleged 'influence of the Zionist lobby on public and political debate',[85] while the former Director of the Centre for Peace and Conflict Studies (CPACS) at the University of Sydney, Professor Stuart Rees, attacked the alleged 'political and financial power' of the pro-Israel lobby.[86] Another BDS campaigner Vacy Vlazna alleged that prominent University of New South Wales academic administrators such as David Gonski and Fred Hilmer, whom she identified as being of Jewish background, were responsible for the establishment of the Israeli-connected Max Brenner chocolate shop on campus.[87]

CPACS Director Associate Professor Jake Lynch took the conspiracy theory even further. In February 2011, Lynch argued in *New Matilda* that the Jewish community was responsible for the Australian Labor Party switching leaders from Kevin Rudd to Julia Gillard on the grounds that Gillard was more supportive of Israel than Rudd.[88] Lynch was implying that Jewish financial influence was a key determinant of ALP Middle East policy. Similarly, Professor Mona Baker of the University of Manchester alleged that global Zionist influence was spreading well beyond Israel to dominate domestic political agendas in the United States and many other Western countries.[89]

Other manifestations of anti-Semitism have included BDS protests against shops such as Starbucks or Marks & Spencer in London simply on the basis that they are Jewish-owned,[90] a BDS protest outside a synagogue in Colorado,[91] and a planned protest outside a synagogue on Shabbat in Melbourne.[92] Additionally, BDS campaigners have made deliberate attempts to diminish and trivialise the extent of Jewish suffering in the Holocaust by comparing Jews with Nazis. The Australians for Palestine group, for example, directly compared Israel's treatment of the Palestinians with the Holocaust, and argued that a failure to boycott Israel was the equivalent of the world's silence concerning Nazi genocide.[93] Similarly, leading BDS advocate Omar Barghouti drew an analogy between Israel's separation fence and the Warsaw ghetto wall, and more broadly between Israeli checkpoints in the West Bank and Nazi actions against Jews.[94]

In an interview with radical left website *Counterpunch*, Roger Waters, a noted BDS campaigner from the iconic rock group 'Pink Floyd', remarked that he

> would not have played for the Vichy government in occupied France in the Second World War, [nor] I would not have played in Berlin either during this time. Many people did, back in the day. There were many people that pretended that the oppression of the Jews was not going on. From 1933 until 1946. So this is not a new scenario. Except that this time it's the Palestinian People being murdered. It's the duty of every thinking human being to ask: "What can I do?"

Demonstrating a remarkable lack of historical awareness Waters then blamed the 'extraordinary' power of the 'Jewish lobby' for the lack of traction BDS had made in the US music industry: 'I promise you, naming no names, I've spoken to people who are terrified that if they stand shoulder to shoulder with me they are going to get fucked. They have said to me "aren't you worried for your life?" and I go "No, I'm not".'[95]

There have also been a number of examples of verbal abuse or threats of violence against those who oppose the BDS movement. Jewish students and staff in London were abused by BDS advocates leading to the resignation of three members of the National Union of Students Executive in protest at the failure of their union to take action against these racist activities.[96] There have been multiple threats of violence including death threats directed at pro-Israel students at the University of Michigan,[97] and there was an attempt led by a prominent anti-Semite to physically prevent an anti-BDS talk at the National University of Ireland in Galway.[98]

These examples of overt bigotry are bad enough. But even if most BDS advocates identify as opponents of racism, the fact remains that the core agenda of the BDS movement is anti-Semitic. As we have already noted, the movement does not seek Israeli–Palestinian peace and reconciliation or the enhancement of Palestinian national and human rights via a two-state solution. Rather, it seeks to eliminate the existing Jewish State of Israel, and replace it with a new national state dominated by an Arab majority, which would become a Greater Palestine.

This means that the approximately 6.135 million Jews living in Israel, who currently constitute 75 per cent of the 8.18 million population of that country,[99] would be completely disenfranchised as a national collective. That is, a country created as a refuge for European Jews who fled or survived Nazi genocide and Middle Eastern Jews who were ethnically cleansed en masse from the Arab world would suddenly cease to exist. At best, many Israeli Jews might become refugees joining the long queue to seek asylum all over the globe. At worst, they could suffer mass violence and genocide.[100] But according to the BDS movement these outcomes would advance human rights rather than anti-Jewish racism.

The BDS movement's opportunistic exploitation of Jews

The BDS movement has falsely implied that Jews are significantly divided on whether or not they support Israel, and cited the pro-BDS opinions of some anti-Zionist Jews as indicating major Jewish support for the BDS movement.

In fact, surveys of Jews in Australia, the United States and the United Kingdom have all confirmed the centrality of Israel to Jewish life and identity.[101] The 2009 survey of Australian Jewry found strong support for Zionism and the State of Israel. Eighty per cent defined themselves as Zionists, and 76 per cent indicated that they felt special concern whenever Israel was in danger. However, there was a diversity of reponses to a question concerning what West Bank settlements Israel should be willing to dismantle in return for peace. Twenty-nine per cent favoured dismantling all or most, 18 per cent supported dismantling some, 32 per cent favoured dismantling few or none, and 21 per cent did not know or declined to answer.[102] Based on this survey and the other international Jewish surveys cited above, we would estimate that about 40–45 per cent of Jews support Israel without qualification, about 50–55 per cent support a two-state solution upholding both Israeli and Palestinian national rights and favour open debate on Israeli policies and less than one per cent hold anti-Zionist views.

It needs to be emphasised that most of the Jews who support two states are strongly committed to the well-being of Israel. In contrast, the anti-Zionist Jews mostly believe in the so-called 'one-state' solution whereby the existing Jewish State of Israel should be eliminated and replaced by an exclusivist Arab State of Greater Palestine in which Jews would be at best tolerated as a religious minority. For the most part, anti-Zionist Jews reject ethnic or cultural connections with the Jewish community, and eschew feelings of solidarity with other Jews who are oppressed or attacked. Their intent is to exclude and censor the views of the vast majority of ordinary Jews.[103] Their viewpoint is not only tiny in Jewish communities worldwide, but also marginal even amongst left-wing Jews.

Despite this, the BDS movement has regularly exaggerated the views of anti-Zionist Jews as reflecting a much wider collection of Jewish opinion.

Omar Barghouti has written about the 'growing support among progressive European and American Jews for effective pressure on Israel'.[104] Elsewhere, he refers to 'principled Jewish voices' supportive of the BDS, and praised the role they play in deflecting what he considers to be unfounded charges of anti-Semitism.[105]

Leading BDS advocates Mona Baker and Lawrence Davidson have referred without evidence to the 'mounting crescendo of Jewish voices against Zionist and Israel colonialist practices'. They allege that many of the 'supporters of the boycott are Jewish'.[106] The Irish BDS activist David Landy proudly cites the support of Jewish anti-Zionist groups such as Independent Jewish Voices Canada and European Jews for a Just Peace for a BDS, but fails to comment on the tiny level of support they receive in their respective Jewish communities.[107] The Irish Academics for Palestine assert that many prominent supporters of the BDS are Jews, and even claim that 'many Jews around the world are distancing themselves from the acts of the Israeli state as a way of reclaiming the Jewish tradition of justice and universality'.[108] No research is provided as proof of this expansive statement.

Similarly, the Israeli academic and BDS activist Ilan Pappe asserts 'that in the last few years the voice of non-Zionist Jews is increasingly heard'.[109] Canadian BDS advocates, academics Abigail Bakan and Yasmeen Abu-Laban, refer to 'new and louder voices in support of boycotting Israel ... among the international Jewish community', and also claim that 'a number of Jewish civil society organisations and prominent individuals have also endorsed the BDS campaign'.[110] But the organisations and individuals they name are overwhelmingly marginal within Jewish communities.

An Australian academic and BDS activist, Ned Curthoys, dubiously argues that 'there is growing support for the BDS from Jews inside and outside Israel', that the BDS movement is 'beginning to seriously fracture the American Jewish community', and that 'leading Jewish intellectuals and activists' – he names prominent anti-Zionists Judith Butler, Naomi Klein, Mike Leigh, Ronnie Kasrils and Richard Falk – support the BDS movement.[111] Two other Australian academics, Paul Duffill and Gabriella Scoff, contend on the basis of little evidence that there has been so much growth in Jewish support for the BDS internationally that 'the question is no longer whether or not to boycott, but rather to what extent do we boycott'.[112] We cite further Australian examples of this disingenuous practice in chapter 3.

So why does the BDS movement highlight the views of this small group of anti-Zionist Jews who are so unrepresentative of collective Jewish opinion? There are two reasons. The first is that it represents a continuation of an unsavoury historical practice. There has been a long history of anti-Semitism in parts of the radical Left whereby a small number of unrepresentative token Jews are opportunistically encouraged to exploit their own religious and cultural origins in order to vilify their own people. This happened in 1929 when American Jewish Communists were obliged to defend the anti-Jewish pogroms in Palestine. It happened again in 1952–53 when Jewish Communists were rolled out to endorse Stalin's anti-Semitic show trial of Rudolf Slánský and his Jewish Communist colleagues in Czechoslovakia, and the Doctors' Plot – when Jewish doctors in Moscow were accused of planning the assassination of Soviet leaders – in the Soviet Union. It has happened many times since 1967 when left-wing Jews have been pressured to publicly conform to the anti-Zionist fundamentalism of the far Left.[113]

Radical Left groups are highly unlikely to employ such techniques against other historically oppressed nations. They would not highlight the views of Indigenous Australians who oppose land rights, or demand that a feminist journal publish the views of women who oppose abortion. They would certainly not publicise the views of Palestinians or Arabs who support Zionism. The contemporary factor is that the BDS movement attempts to use Jewish anti-Zionists as an alibi against serious accusations of anti-Semitism by arguing that Jews also share their views.[114] A Jewish member of the American Studies Association (and defender of its pro-BDS motion) has even claimed that the BDS movement cannot possibly be anti-Semitic because it is supported by some Jewish academics.[115] But this transparent strategy is easily exposed by anti-racists.

The left-wing UK scholar David Hirsh has noted in relation to the participation of a small number of anti-Zionist Jews in the British campaign for an academic boycott of Israel, 'Jews too can make anti-Semitic claims, use anti-Semitic images, support anti-Semitic exclusions and play an important, if unwitting, part in preparing the ground for the future emergence of an anti-Semitic movement'.[116] Indeed, Jewish anti-Zionist individuals and groups have defended racist arguments such as the allegation that Jews collaborated with the Nazis to perpetrate the Holocaust, or that Israel is perpetrating similar crimes to the Nazis, or that a Jewish lobby controls the international media.[117]

Does BDS target institutions or individuals?

The BDS movement has generally insisted that the boycott is directed only at institutional arrangements with Israeli universities and does not adversely impact on individual academics. They have also strenuously denied that the boycott involves a McCarthyist form of blacklisting.[118] In 2011, the Palestinian BDS National Committee emphasised that BDS activities do not target 'specifically businesses with Israeli ownership, based on the nationality of their owner. Businesses and institutions are rather chosen based on their direct contribution to grave human rights abuses and international law violations of the Israeli state and military, or to rebranding campaigns that attempt to whitewash Israel's crimes'.[119] A further 2013 statement by the Committee stated that 'BDS does not call for a boycott of individuals because she or he happens to be Israeli or because they express certain views'.[120] Similarly, Australian BDS activist Kim Bullimore claims that the movement targets only Israeli government bodies and institutions rather than individual citizens.[121]

At the very least, these statements are intentionally ambiguous and vague since they can be applied to just about every Israeli organisation that does not support the BDS agenda, and the overwhelming majority of Israeli citizens who are associated with those organisations. As noted by British sociologist Robert Fine, they fail to distinguish between civil society organisations including universities and the state, and attempt to hold Israeli academics collectively responsible for state actions.[122] They also ignore the innate link between individual academics and the universities that employ and support their work whilst obscuring the fact that it is individuals (or research teams) that produce intellectual output, not the universities. It is individual Israeli academics who will inevitably be denied opportunities to travel to international conferences, to develop inter-collegial relationships, and to participate in inter-institutional research projects. It is their academic freedom that will be infringed.[123]

Elsewhere, the Palestinian Campaign for the Cultural and Academic Boycott of Israel (PACBI) has revealed that any individual who represents the state of Israel or any Israeli organisation, or is involved in any attempts to defend Israeli policies, should be subject to the same boycott measures as an Israeli institution.[124] They add that individual academics should not be exempted from boycotts if they undertake a 'particularly offensive act or statement'. Examples given are 'direct or indirect incitement to violence; justification – an indirect form of advocacy – of war crimes and other grave violations of international law; racial slurs; and actual participation in human rights violations'.[125] These accusations imply that any Israeli academic who has ever participated in actions of the Israeli army to defend Israel and its citizens against violence or terror deserves to be boycotted.

It is, therefore, hardly surprising that there are numerous examples of the black-banning of individual Israeli academics and scholars. We have already referred to the exclusionary actions of Mona Baker in Manchester who sacked two Israeli academics from her Editorial Board on the basis of their nationality, not their views. She added that she would not consider any articles from Israeli researchers for her journal.[126] Another case involved Professor Andrew Wilkie from Oxford University who refused on political grounds to employ an Israeli research student in his laboratory. Wilkie was later suspended by the university without pay for two months and ordered to undertake equal opportunities training.[127] A further case occurred at a South African Sociological Association conference in 2012 when an Israeli sociologist, who refused a demand to condemn 'Israeli apartheid', was boycotted by other participants and forced to present his paper to an empty room.[128] In September 2013, the British trade union Unison allegedly vetoed a scheduled conflict-resolution workshop by Israeli academic Moty Cristal on the grounds of his Israeli nationality.[129] And in August 2014, the pro-BDS far Left MP for Bradford West George Galloway went even further by demanding that not only Israeli academics but also Israeli tourists be excluded from the city of Bradford.[130]

Additionally, there is an obvious risk of McCarthyism. A report by the American Association of University Professors warned against the use of political or religious tests as a basis for participation in academic debate.[131] Even the pro-BDS American academic Judith Butler acknowledged that proposals for 'discrimination on the basis of political viewpoints' provoked reasonable 'fears of a renewed McCarthyism'.[132] But as noted in chapter 4, the British AUT's April 2005 boycott motion included a reference to exempt 'good' Israeli academics who condemned the policies of their own country, and conformed to a test of political orthodoxy. Similarly, NATFHE's 2006 resolution suggested an exemption for academics who publicly dissociated themselves from Israeli government policies.[133] The long-time British Jewish Marxist Steve Cohen called this an horrific example of a 'loyalty test' designed to impose 'collective guilt' on Jews,[134] whilst the late left-wing Israeli academic Baruch Kimmerling said he would 'not cooperate with any institution or person' who used 'non-academic criteria' to select which academics deserved to be included or excluded.[135]

Strengthening the Israeli Right

The BDS movement's targeting of Israeli academics undermines the most liberal group in Israeli society, which includes a significant number of dissidents who are willing to challenge government policies and support Palestinian rights.[136] To be sure, Israeli academics are as heterogeneous as any other academic community, and many are apolitical or remain silent. But a significant minority of academics is active in organisations that oppose the West Bank occupation, and 358 Israeli academics signed a petition supporting conscientious draft objectors who refused to serve in the West Bank.[137] Baruch Kimmerling called the Israeli academy 'the last bastion of free thought and free speech', and argued that they had behaved far more responsibly than academic communities elsewhere (such as England and America) at times of war or internal political repression.[138]

But instead of engaging with these dissident forces in Israel, which are frequently under attack from Israeli hawks, the BDS movement seeks to exclude them. These actions only reinforce the siege mentality of many Israelis and strengthen the right-wing forces in Israel who are opposed to peaceful negotiations and a two-state solution.[139] The long-time Israeli peacenik Naomi Chazan calls the movement a 'boomerang' that aids the 'far right' by convincing many Israelis 'that the entire world is against us'.[140] Similarly, the left-wing American author Eric Alterman accuses the movement of weakening the Israeli academics and cultural figures that are most likely to favour compromise.[141] Another left-wing Israeli academic David Newman, who has engaged in numerous joint research projects with Palestinian counterparts, comments that the BDS 'strengthens the rejectionists on both sides' and directly precludes the dialogue and co-operation necessary to 'build practical or political foundations for peace'.[142]

In this chapter, we have identified the BDS movement as rejectionists who support a return to the earlier pre-1993 Palestinian position in favour of the elimination of Israel. The movement explicitly supports the one-state solution and seeks to exclude Israelis, on the basis of their nationality not their views, from international discourse. The movement directs much of its anger precisely at those left-wing Israelis, Jews and others who in contrast endorse Israeli-Palestinian peace and reconciliation leading to a two-state solution. This much is demonstrated by our two case studies.

3

Case study:
BDS in Australia

Australian Jewry – home to one of the world's largest Holocaust survivor populations[1] – makes up only a small percentage of the nation's population. Australia's economic, political and cultural links with Israel are arguably minor, certainly in comparison with the United States and Europe. Yet BDS activists have been a conspicuous presence in recent years triggering several political controversies and regularly attracting the ire of the local Jewish population and its communal leadership and garnering global attention, particularly from Israel. As a wealthy Western liberal democracy with a relatively influential Jewish diaspora, and an increasingly assertive diaspora Arab lobby, Australia is a frontline nation for BDS activists. Given the tendency of BDS campaigns to polarise relations between pro-Israel and pro-Palestinian communities, they may pose a serious threat to Australia's multicultural harmony.

This chapter examines the key manifestations of BDS activities in Australia including the academic boycott petition, the Max Brenner protests, the University of Sydney Centre for Peace and Conflict Studies, pro-Palestinian advocacy groups such as Australians for Palestine, Jewish anti-Zionist groups and sections of the Greens and the trade union movement. Other than the boycott petition, all these activities took place in the period from 2009 onwards as a reaction to the specific conflicts between Israel and Hamas. Most of the key Australian individuals and groups involved conform to the general extremist perspective of the global BDS movement: they favour a one-state rather than a two-state solution, they are only concerned with Palestinian and not Israeli national and human rights, they engage in ethnic stereotyping of all Israeli Jews, they are hostile to two-state advocates and they actively exaggerate and exploit the presence of a small number of Jews in the movement in an attempt to deflect serious allegations of anti-Semitism stemming from their activities. As such, BDS activists in Australia have merely contributed to the already poisonous nature of much of the debate around Israel-Palestine.

The 2002 academic boycott petition

The first incarnation of BDS activity in Australia was the academic boycott petition of May 2002 initiated by two well-known left-of-centre academics, John Docker of the Australian National University and Ghassan Hage of the University of Sydney. Both have a public record of hardline criticism of Israel.[2] The Australian petition seemed to merely copy the boycott call initiated by Steven and Hilary Rose in Britain one month earlier, and was arguably based on the binary opposites of good and bad nations. It made the following key points:

- While the Palestinians are rightly requested to rein in their extremists, the Israelis have elected their extremists to power.
- Israel has perpetrated ugly murder, rampages, systematic crimes of war and an anachronistic act of colonisation in the West Bank and Gaza.
- Israel is impervious to moral appeals from world leaders.
- While some academics and intellectuals in Israel oppose the government and some also are involved in co-operative Israeli–Palestinian research projects, the vast majority have either supported the Israeli Army's onslaught on the Palestinians, or failed to voice any significant protest against it.
- As with boycotts against apartheid South Africa, international action is now required to stop the massacres perpetrated against the Palestinian people.
- We call for a boycott of research and cultural links with Israel. We urge our colleagues not to attend conferences in Israel, to pressure our universities to suspend any existing exchange

or linkage arrangements, and to refuse to distribute scholarship and academic position information.[3]

The petition was signed by more than 90 Australian academics from a range of disciplines in the humanities and social sciences covering about half of Australia's academic institutions. Some were of Arab background and a small number were Jewish. Some were well known for endorsing anti-Zionist fundamentalist positions, whilst others had no previous record of expressing views on the Middle East. Few of the signatories were prominent public intellectuals.[4] The overwhelming majority of Australian academics shunned the petition.

The petition made national headlines but had little impact other than provoking a counter-petition signed by more than 200 academics, which argued against a boycott on the grounds of intellectual freedom and co-operation. The statement made no attempt to rebuke the arguments contained in the boycott petition, noting that its signatories 'hold diverse political views with respect to the past and current policies of the Israeli Government'. Some of the signatories were unqualified supporters of Israel, but others were supporters of the Israeli peace movement and strong opponents of the then Likud-dominated Israeli Government.[5] The vice-chancellors of the University of Sydney and the Australian National University both condemned the academic boycott petition.[6] The then

Coalition Federal Minister for Education, Brendan Nelson, and the Multicultural Affairs Minister, Gary Hardgrave, also denounced the academic boycott petition. Hardgrave called the petition racist and 'a form of censorship at its very worst'.[7] Additionally, unlike the experience of Britain explored in the next chapter, the peak body of Australian academics, the National Tertiary Education Union (NTEU), stated that they would not be endorsing any boycott proposal.[8] This early, principled decision by the union's leadership would seriously set back BDS activism within the academy.

The Max Brenner
chocolate shop protests

In contrast to the short-lived academic boycott initiative, the most aggressive and ongoing Australian BDS activity has been the angry and sometimes violent protests against the Max Brenner chocolate shop in Melbourne and other capital cities. The protesters typically chant extreme anti-Israel slogans, absurdly accusing Max Brenner of supporting the 'displacement, torture and genocide of Palestinians', and urging the restoration of Palestine from 'the river to the sea' (from the Jordan River to the Mediterranean Sea), which is an explicit call for the elimination of the State of Israel. They also scream 'Come off it Max Brenner, there is blood in your chocolate' which some have interpreted as a reference to the ancient racist blood libel alleging that Jews kill Christian babies for religious purposes.[9]

These protests are led by a small group of far-left extremists from the Socialist Alternative organisation who have attempted to physically prevent shoppers from entering the Brenner stores, resulting in a number of arrests. Such tactics arguably eclipse those of BDS protesters elsewhere in the world who have typically eschewed violence. Beginning in December 2010, the protests have targeted the store on the basis that the Israeli-owned parent company, the Strauss Group, provides food and care packages and leisure equipment to Israeli soldiers.[10] Yet the Australian Max Brenner stores are owned by two Australian citizens of Israeli background via a franchise arrangement and even the protesters have admitted that there is no direct connection between the stores and the Israeli army.

The protests have been widely condemned by leading members of the Australian Labor Party and the (conservative) Liberal–National Coalition.[11] Victorian and national Liberal Party MPs led an anti-BDS rally,[12] and a number of prominent national Labor Party figures, including former Prime Minister Kevin Rudd, Deputy Prime Minister Wayne Swan and Ministers Stephen Conroy and David Feeney, visited Max Brenner shops for hot chocolate 'sit-ins' to demonstrate their opposition to the BDS.[13] Rudd said: 'I am here because I object to the boycotting of Jewish businesses'.[14] On another occasion, he condemned 'campaigns against businesses which happen to be owned by members of the Jewish community'.[15] Prime Minister Julia Gillard attacked the protests against Max Brenner, emphasising that Australia supported a two-state solution, and welcomed links between Australian and Israeli researchers and universities.[16] Leading trade union official Paul Howes, then national secretary of the Australian Workers Union, denounced the protesters as 'mimicking the behaviour of Nazi thugs',[17] and argued that it was 'distasteful that a Jewish business is being targeted in this way ... If people are upset about the handling of the Middle East process then fine, but why don't they protest outside the Israeli embassy and direct their protest to the Israeli state rather than a Jewish business?'[18]

The Max Brenner protests seem to symbolise both the extremist politics of the BDS movement and the increasing convergence of anti-Zionist and anti-Jewish messages. For many Jews, this indiscriminate attempt to boycott a Jewish-owned business is frighteningly reminiscent of the Nazi boycott of Jewish commerce in the 1930s. Even the left-wing Australian Jewish Democratic Society (AJDS), which supports a targeted boycott of Israeli settlement products, issued a strong condemnation of the Max Brenner protests as unduly 'confrontational' and 'resonant with anti-Jewish activities in Europe during the 1930s'.[19] Concerns about the racist motives of some protesters were also accentuated by the overt anti-Semitic messages contained in a Facebook page established to support protests against a Max Brenner store being constructed at the University of New South Wales during 2013.[20]

Additionally, the protests seem to present another example of the BDS movement's ongoing ethnic stereotyping of all Israeli Jews as evil given that military service is mandatory in Israel, and there is no evidence that the Strauss Group, let alone its Australian franchisee, has supplied military equipment or supported Israeli settlements in the West Bank.[21] The implication of the protests is that Israel has no right to an army or to defend itself.

Regardless, the Max Brenner protests have drawn public attention to the Palestinian cause. The protests attained wide publicity, and the subsequent court trial of some protesters resulting in trespassing charges being dismissed gained further publicity.[22] The protesters would probably regard this outcome as a success for their cause. However, their fanatical views and strategies are likely to alienate public opinion and indelibly associate the Palestinian narrative with an extremist image.

Centre for Peace and Conflict Studies?

The Centre for Peace and Conflict Studies (CPACS) at the University of Sydney has been a key body in the Australian BDS movement, and at the forefront of activities that attempt to demonise the State of Israel and all those Australians who defend its right to exist. The Centre was formed in May 1988 to promote interdisciplinary research and teaching on the causes of conflict and the conditions that affect conflict resolution and peace. Although the Centre is structurally independent with its own elected Council and Constitution, which includes a specific advocacy directive, it nevertheless still relies on core commonwealth government funding grants, and is formally accountable for its research and teaching outcomes to the Faculty of Arts and Social Sciences at the University of Sydney. However, many of its activities seem to involve participation in partisan political agendas and campaigns such as the BDS, which are not supported by either Faculty or University policy.

From its beginning, CPACS seems to have adopted a simplistic 'good or bad nations' view of Israel-Palestine. Their aim does not appear to be to support compromise or reconciliation, but rather to impose pariah status on Israeli Jews. In addition, they seem to have labelled any and all supporters of Israel – whatever their diverse views on solutions to the conflict – as apologists for the oppression of Palestinians.

This labelling has been particularly apparent in two activities: the awarding of the Sydney Peace Prize by the CPACS-affiliated Sydney Peace Foundation to a number of committed anti-Zionists, and active participation in the BDS movement. Winners of the Sydney Peace Prize over the past decade include the Palestinian intellectual Dr Hanan Ashrawi (2003) who is a relatively pragmatic

Palestinian nationalist but certainly not a peace activist, and anti-Zionist fundamentalists such as John Pilger (2009) and Noam Chomsky (2011). When confronted with criticism, CPACS have tended to revert to anti-Jewish stereotypes. At the time of the controversy over the awarding of the Peace Prize to Ashrawi, CPACS Director Professor Stuart Rees argued on a number of occasions that the Jewish lobby (or what he called 'influential sections of the Jewish community') was 'one of the most powerful lobbies in the world',[23] and had used 'formidable financial power'[24] to protest the decision. He added: 'We are being threatened by members of a powerful group who think they have an entitlement to tell others what to do'.[25]

These arguments were both inaccurate and prejudiced. They were inaccurate since this seemingly all-powerful lobby failed to either reverse the decision to award the peace prize to Ashrawi, or to persuade the then NSW Labor Party Premier Bob Carr not to present the award to Ashrawi. (Indeed, efforts to lobby Premier Carr proved disastrously counterproductive and planted the seeds of a bitter conflict between elements of the Jewish community and the future minister for foreign affairs.) They were prejudiced since they characterised all Jews as comprising a powerful and united lobby, reminiscent of historical far Right allegations that Jews control the world (a 'case' based on the fraudulent Protocols of the Elders of Zion document).

Rees was succeeded as Director of CPACS in

2007 by a little-known UK journalist Jake Lynch. Lynch's fundamentalist distaste for Zionism and Israel was articulated in detail in his 2008 book *Debates in Peace Journalism*. Lynch, too, presented a binary view of the Israeli–Palestinian conflict. He critiqued media reporting of Palestinian terrorism against Israeli civilians, arguing instead for a mode of reporting that favoured the Palestinian narrative of innocent victimhood including their extremist demand for the return of millions of 1948 refugees to Green Line Israel. He also implied that a powerful Jewish lobby in Britain was responsible for the Blair Labour Government's pro-Israel orientation.[26]

As CPACS Director, Lynch quickly took a leadership role in the Australian BDS movement. CPACS has hosted a number of pro-BDS seminars featuring anti-Zionist fundamentalists such as John Docker and Antony Loewenstein, and in 2009 initiated a specific call for a boycott by Sydney University of the Hebrew University of Jerusalem, and the Technion University in Haifa.[27]

In February 2011, Lynch took the critique of the Jewish lobby to a new level. In an astounding article in *New Matilda*, he espoused the conspiracy theory that the Jewish community was responsible for the Australian Labor Party switching leaders from Kevin Rudd to Julia Gillard during June 2010 on the grounds that Gillard was more supportive of Israel than Rudd.[28] The article was both absurd and prejudiced. It was absurd because there was not the slightest difference between Rudd and Gillard in their fundamental support for Israel, and many commentators have documented a multitude of influential factors that forced the ALP to overthrow Rudd.

It was prejudiced because it suggested – quoting an earlier superficial argument from *Sydney Morning Herald* journalist Peter Hartcher[29] – that Jewish financial influence was a key determinant of ALP's Middle East policy. Yet Lynch has not conducted any empirical analysis of which Jews contribute to the ALP as major donors, what business or political agendas they seek to progress via their donations, whether or not they have any particular interest in Israel, and how their donations compare to those emanating from other ethnic interest groups such as Chinese Australians, Lebanese Australians, mining lobbyists and so on. Short of any such analysis, his theory seems to be simply another variant of the old far-right argument that Jews hold disproportionate financial power and wealth, which enables them to control political parties and governments.

In an attempt to deflect allegations of anti-Semitism, Lynch and his colleagues continually point to a number of Jewish visitors hosted by CPACS, and disingenuously attempt to imply that there is major Jewish support for the BDS. But these Jewish alibis of CPACS are nearly all extreme anti-Zionist Jews – such as Docker, Loewenstein, Chomsky, American BDS activist Anna Baltzer, and Israelis Ilan Pappe, Uri Davis and Jeff Halper.[30] While the Jewishness of these figures is clearly secondary to their left-wing political identity they are, ironically, frequently willing to exploit their own religious and cultural origins in order to vilify the Jewish community and individual Jewish political opponents. Former CPACS Director Stuart Rees, who still chairs the Sydney Peace Foundation, expediently claimed that 'many prominent Jewish citizens' in Australia plus 'members of organizations like Independent Jewish Voices are significant BDS supporters'.[31] This statement vastly exaggerates the tiny number of anti-Zionist Australian Jews who endorse the BDS.

As with other BDS advocates, CPACS have claimed that the boycott is only directed at Israeli institutions, not at individuals on the basis of their Israeli or Jewish identity.[32] But it is apparent that this tolerance is only directed at hardline anti-Zionist Jews who pass a McCarthyist test of anti-Zionist political orthodoxy. In early 2013, Lynch refused an offer to collaborate with Professor Dan Avnon, a Hebrew University political scientist who is renowned as the only Israeli scholar to draft national civics curriculums that are aimed jointly at both Jewish and Arab children. Despite the fact that Avnon is precisely the type of moderate Israeli that is involved in combating intolerance and promoting peace and conflict resolution, Lynch refused contact on the grounds that Avnon is affiliated with an Israeli university.[33]

The Vice-Chancellor of the University of Sydney strongly rejected the call by CPACS to boycott Israeli academic institutions.[34] Additionally, Lynch's boycott of Avnon provoked a law suit from an Israeli non-government law centre, Shurat HaDin, which alleged that Lynch had infringed the *Racial Discrimination Act 1975* by targeting Avnon on the basis of his nationality. CPACS and their supporters responded by arguing that the legal action was an unfair attempt to restrict their freedom of speech. Leading Australian Jewish organisations critical of the BDS movement, such as the Executive Council of Australian Jewry, chose not to support the court case on the grounds that it was likely to be counter-productive. The lawsuit collapsed in July 2014 on technical grounds that no plaintiffs were willing to appear in the Australian court.[35]

CPACS have clearly enjoyed some superficial success in drawing public attention to the BDS movement although most of the mainstream media reporting of their activities has been hostile. Regardless, they seem to have had little influence on other academics. The national NTEU remains firmly opposed to the BDS, and no other social science or humanities associations or university departments have adopted the BDS cause. It is also possible that CPACS fanaticism has actively discouraged Jewish students or academics from entering the peace studies field despite their obvious interest in reconciling Jewish/Israeli and Palestinian/Arab perspectives.

The Australian Greens

Endorsement by sections of the Australian Greens is arguably the most significant political gain by the local BDS movement. The Australian Greens is the parliamentary political party that is most closely associated with the Palestinian cause. A number of current and former federal Greens senators have made statements sharply critical of Israeli policies.[36] Nevertheless, the federal party nationally still supports a two-state solution and it rejected a BDS proposal at its March 2010 conference. Leading Greens figures including consecutive federal party leaders Bob Brown and Christine Milne, former long-standing NSW Greens MP Ian Cohen, and current NSW State MPs Jan Barham, Cate Faehrmann and Jeremy Buckingham have all voiced opposition to a BDS.[37]

However, strong support for a BDS emanates from the NSW Branch of the Greens including the elected national senator for NSW and former activist in the far left Socialist Party, Lee Rhiannon, the former NSW Greens State MP Sylvia Hale, some current elected members of the NSW State Parliament such as John Kaye and David Shoebridge, and a number of elected local councillors. Both Rhiannon and Shoebridge have publicly defended the Max Brenner protests. As recently as December 2013, Rhiannon called on Australia to cease all military co-operation and trade with Israel.[38]

The NSW Greens passed a pro-BDS motion in December 2010. One week later, the Greens-controlled Inner-West Marrickville Council adopted an official policy of boycotting Israel. The motion was also supported by the four ALP councillors and one independent councillor, and passed by ten votes to two. The Greens Mayor, Fiona Byrne, promised to campaign for a state-wide ban on contact with Israel if she was elected to State Parliament at the 2011 election. It is possible that this vote reflected a pragmatic concern to attract Arab voters in the electorate as much as political idealism.[39]

But the Marrickville boycott proposal provoked considerable controversy and opposition. The Labor Prime Minister Julia Gillard called the proposed Marrickville Council boycott 'stupid and repugnant', adding that 'Israel is a democracy with whom we have a long-standing relationship'.[40] The local Labor federal member, cabinet minister in the Gillard government and senior left faction leader, Anthony Albanese, also attacked the Marrickville boycott, urging 'sensible solutions and understanding' to promote Israeli-Palestinian peace, 'not counter-productive self-indulgence'.[41]

In March 2011, the Australian Senate passed an anti-BDS motion proposed by Senator Mitch Fifield of the Coalition. The motion acknowledged 'that Israel is a legitimate and democratic state and a good friend of Australia; and denounces the Israel boycott by the Marrickville Council and condemns any expansion of it'.[42] The motion was supported by all representatives of the Coalition and Labor Party, but opposed by Senator Bob Brown of the Greens. Similarly, the Chair of the Ethnic Communities Council of NSW, Jack Passaris, strongly opposed Marrickville Council's BDS proposal on the grounds that it would undermine the 'principles of multiculturalism'.[43]

Fiona Byrne's subsequent failure to win the seat of Marrickville in the state election was widely attributed to her advocacy of BDS.[44] Later, the Marrickville Council voted in April 2011 to abandon the campaign due to fears that implementing a BDS would cost taxpayers up to $4 million, and an associated concern that the Council was neglecting its core local services and functions.[45] However the Council passed a motion, which whilst rejecting formal support for the BDS movement, still endorsed the three key BDS objectives.[46] In November 2011, the NSW Greens replaced their existing pro-BDS policy with a more moderate and ambiguous motion that recognised the 'legitimacy of BDS as a political tactic', but acknowledged that the Party held a 'diversity of views' on the issue.[47]

A number of NSW Greens have made exaggerated statements implying that the BDS movement has widespread Jewish support. Lee Rhiannon claimed that 'many Jewish communities support this work',[48] whilst Fiona Byrne alleged 'a growing number of Jews' support the BDS.[49] In fact, the only organised Jewish community group in Marrickville, the Inner West Jewish Community and Friends

Peace Alliance, which is left-oriented and strongly supportive of a two-state solution, devoted considerable time and resources to opposing the Marrickville BDS proposal. Strangely, Byrne admitted in a meeting with the Alliance that she did not even know a Jewish community existed in Marrickville despite the fact that there has been a synagogue in Newtown since 1918.[50]

The poor showing of Greens Party candidates at the March 2011 NSW state election and the subsequent abandonment of the earlier pro-BDS motion constituted a major setback for BDS activists in Australia. It also confirms our concern that the BDS movement promotes the exclusion of most Jews from progressive movements and parties, and actively divides progressive communities on the basis of attitudes to one foreign policy issue, which happens to have little direct political relevance to Australia. These divisions then undermine progressive unity around other more pressing concerns that can be practically addressed such as the current national Coalition Government's cuts to university funding, Indigenous programs and social welfare services and payments, and the increasingly hardline policies on asylum seekers.

Jewish support for the BDS

The BDS movement has disingenuously implied significant Jewish opposition to Israel by highlighting the views of hardline anti-Zionists such as John Docker, Peter Slezak and Antony Loewenstein. But in fact, the Australian Jewish community including many left-wing Jews who are critical of the West Bank settlements, overwhelmingly opposes the BDS. Limited support has come only from small left-wing groups such as the Australian Jewish Democratic Society (AJDS), and the even smaller Jews Against the Occupation and Independent Australian Jewish Voices (IAJV). One of the two spokespersons for IAJV, Dr Peter Slezak, acknowledged that Australian Jews 'who support the BDS are a small, unrepresentative minority'.[51]

The AJDS, formed in 1984, was historically a strong supporter of the two-state solution,[52] but has in recent years adopted a more ambiguous position concerning conflict resolution. In August 2010, AJDS voted in favour of a limited boycott of Israeli settlement products from outside the June 1967 borders. It rejected any blanket BDS campaign against Israel including the core BDS demand for a Palestinian Right of Return, but nevertheless still used the language of the BDS movement to endorse selective campaigns aimed at ending Israel's occupation of the West Bank. The motion was passed following an invited address to AJDS members by Samah Sabawi, a representative of the pro-BDS Australians for Palestine group. Most members of AJDS agreed with the fundamentals of her argument, but expressed strong disagreement with her use of the term 'apartheid state' to describe Israel.[53]

The former AJDS President, Harold Zwier, later resigned from the AJDS Executive due to his concern that the motion had aligned the AJDS with the global BDS movement's agenda for eliminating Israel.[54]

AJDS maintained an ambiguous approach to the BDS. In September 2011, the organisation denounced local BDS protests held against the Israeli-linked Max Brenner chocolate company on the grounds that they were unduly confrontational, and directed by groups favouring the elimination of the State of Israel.[55] But in March 2013, AJDS once again advocated a limited boycott campaign aimed at settlement products. They denied that the campaign was in any way linked to the aims or objectives of the global BDS movement, or that it was hostile to the State of Israel.[56] However, a leading member of the AJDS Executive, Jordy Silverstein, quickly clarified that she personally supported the three core aims of the BDS agenda, which are intended to delegitimise and ultimately eliminate Israel.[57] AJDS's support of targeted BDS activities has been strongly rejected by Jewish communal roof bodies such as the Jewish Community Council of Victoria (JCCV) (which includes AJDS as an affiliate) and the Executive Council of Australian Jewry.[58] Nevertheless, BDS activists who don't share AJDS's emphasis on a limited boycott, have enthusiastically publicised the organisation's endorsement of the BDS and drawn particular attention to its affiliation to the mainstream JCCV.[59]

Trade unions

There has been very little union support for the BDS in Australia compared to Britain or even Canada. The Australian Council of Trade Unions and most of its members support a two-state solution and oppose the BDS movement in accordance with the views of the International Trade Union Confederation. The Australian Workers Union played an active role alongside trade unions in the USA and Canada in forming TULIP – Trade Unions Linking Israel and Palestine. TULIP favours co-operation between the Israeli Histadrut (Labour Council) and the Palestinian General Federation of Trade Unions as a pathway to peace and reconciliation.[60] As we explored earlier, Australia's National Tertiary Education Union has also continued to reject pro-BDS motions.[61]

Support for the BDS has been limited to a small number of left-wing unions, and an informal pro-Palestinian union network called AusPalestine or Australian Unionists Supporting Palestine has been formed to co-ordinate these activities.[62] But some of the unions involved, such as the Construction, Forestry, Mining and Energy Union (CFMEU) and the Australian Manufacturing Workers Union (AMWU) still claim to support two states, and only endorse a partial BDS targeted at the West Bank settlements.[63] There seems to have been little active union support for the BDS except from one or two state branches.

However, the Left-dominated Victorian Trades Hall Council (VTHC), which was headed at the time by Maritime Union of Australia official Kevin Bracken who promotes a conspiracy view of the 11 September 2001 attacks on the United States, hosted a BDS conference in October 2010. The keynote speaker was the visiting American BDS activist, Anna Baltzer, who favours the abolition of the State of Israel and its replacement by an Arab State of Greater Palestine. Five Australian unions sent official delegations to this conference. But the VTHC's pro-BDS position was condemned by David Cragg, a leading moderate unionist and Assistant Secretary of the Council.[64] A further VTHC motion passed in August 2011 also supported the BDS movement.[65] But overall the BDS movement has attracted little interest and minimum support and resources from the Australian union movement. In contrast to Britain, the BDS has not been a divisive factor in individual unions.

Pro-Palestinian advocacy groups

Three pro-Palestinian advocacy groups have been active supporters of the BDS movement: Australians for Palestine (AFP), The Coalition for Justice and Peace in Palestine (CJPP), and the Australia Palestine Advocacy Network (APAN).

The hardline AFP, which is headed by long-standing Australian Palestinian lobbyist Sonja Karkar and employs three full-time staff,[66] supports the three key objectives of the BDS movement which would inevitably lead to a Greater Palestine in place of Israel.[67] The AFP is active in organising BDS events and supporting the BDS in public forums and the media. AFP has actively defended the Max Brenner protests and disingenuously claims that 'many Jews support BDS'.[68] The CJPP, headed by long-time anti-Zionist campaigners Antony Loewenstein and Peter Manning, shares the hardline views of AFP, and works closely with the Centre for Peace and Conflict Studies.

In contrast, the relatively moderate APAN, which is supported by a number of churches and trade unions, supports the BDS in principle and hosts visiting BDS activists, but also endorses two states and has condemned the aggressive nature of the Max Brenner protests.[69] The Palestinian Ambassador to Australia, Izzat Abdulhadi, has also condemned the Max Brenner protests, and rejected any blanket BDS given that the Palestinian Authority supports a two-state solution.[70]

Some churches have supported a targeted boycott aimed at West Bank settlements. The National Council of Churches – a coalition of 19 Protestant congregations – recommended in August 2010 that its 'member Churches and the wider Australian community consider a boycott of goods produced by Israeli settlements in the Occupied Palestinian territories'. The Executive Council of Australian Jewry strongly rejected this proposal.[71] Additionally, one of the strongest supporters of the BDS in Marrickville has been Father Dave Smith from the Holy Trinity Anglican Church, and support has also come from the social justice committee of the St Brigid's Catholic Church.[72] These Christian pro-BDS manifestations seem minor compared to the anti-Israel campaigns of progressive churches in the United States, United Kingdom and Canada. However, they confirm the potential of the BDS movement to provoke enmity between different religious as well as ethnic communities.

———

The BDS campaign has made little headway in the Australian mainstream. Both the conservative Liberal–National Party Coalition and the Australian Labor Party have consistently opposed the BDS movement. The then Shadow Foreign Affairs Spokesperson (and now Minister for Foreign Affairs) Julie Bishop even promised to remove research funding from any academic individuals or institutions who support the BDS campaign,[73] although in government the Coalition Government does not seem to have honoured this promise.

To be sure, left-wing Labor Party MP Melissa Parke became in October 2014 the first non-Greens member of the national parliament to support the BDS movement. Citing anti-Zionist Jews such as Peter Slezak and Israeli-born Marcelo Svirsky, she denied that the BDS was either anti-Semitic or favoured the destruction of Israel whilst ignoring significant evidence to the contrary.[74] However, ALP leader Bill Shorten firmly rejected her pro-BDS position and reaffirmed the ALP's support for Israel.[75]

In contrast to the United Kingdom and the United States, no high-profile academics, media figures, political activists, union leaders, religious leaders or actors have voiced support for the BDS, and no Australian companies or banks appear to have divested from Israeli products. Support for the BDS has been largely limited to the margins including some Greens politicians, radical Left activists and little-known academics. The BDS movement seems to be supported only by the extreme fringe of those who are concerned with Palestinian national and human rights. Most BDS advocates in Australia are ideological extremists who support a blanket BDS based on the ethnic stereotyping of all Israeli Jews as an evil, oppressor nation. Their political strategy is to turn Israel into a pariah state, which can be effectively excluded from the international community. A minority of Australian BDS supporters claim to endorse two states and naively endorse a targeted BDS despite the fact that the global BDS movement explicitly seeks the elimination of the State of Israel rather than merely an end to the West Bank occupation. None of the BDS advocates provide any practical plan for advancing Israeli-Palestinian peace and reconciliation. Rather, their sole focus is on demonising Israel, while ignoring the existence of Palestinian/ Arab violence and extremism. It is a familiar story.

4

Case study: BDS in Britain and North America

The 'Global' Boycott, Divestments and Sanctions movement is in many respects a misnomer. Most of the world's population is ambivalent towards BDS, or blissfully unaware of its existence. Indeed, the campaign's viability lives or dies on the basis of its activities in North America and key European nations. Without the efforts of Western-based Palestinian campaigners and their supporters the call to boycott Israel allegedly issued on behalf of Palestinian civil society in 2004 would have suffered political stillbirth.

This chapter explores the progress of BDS in Britain and North America. Our focus here is on the academy and progressive bodies such as trade unions, but the chapter also considers examples of prominent individuals, churches and companies who have chosen to support (or reject) BDS, even if partially. As we shall see, no government in the world has signed up to BDS. A handful of unions have joined, but no significant confederations. No universities and very few noteworthy scholarly organisations support BDS. There has been a recent spike in the number of companies divesting from Israeli enterprises but these companies have done so only in regard to activities in the occupied West Bank. A blanket boycott of Israeli academic, cultural and economic institutions seems a forlorn hope.

To be sure, the activities of BDS supporters have done little to assist the stalled peace process between Israel and the Palestinians. American and British individuals and groups have merely perpetuated the extremist perspective of the global BDS movement around the promotion of a one-state rather than a two-state solution. BDS has not improved the quality of life of a single Palestinian or Israeli, or fostered dialogue between diaspora groupings. The one substantive outcome arising from the formal campaign in North America and Britain has been the fostering of divisive and unproductive public debates, sometimes accompanied by anti-Semitic outbursts, as well as spurring intra-union and community conflict. Additionally, pro-BDS campaigns have directly led to the departure of Jews from a number of progressive organisations, a type of dual tragedy. By most objective measures, BDS has reaped a bitter harvest.

The early years of BDS, 2002–2008

The years following the formal BDS call-to-arms are best seen as akin to a phoney war. The movement could claim very few 'successes' in the West between 2004 and 2008. Arguably, the attention of Western politicians and their citizens, including left-wing activists, was directed towards the fallout from the 2003 American-led invasion of Iraq. This is to say nothing of the associated debate around the 'war on terror' that followed the 11 September 2001 terrorist attacks upon American soil that prompted a Western coalition to launch a military intervention in Afghanistan.

Granted, there were some major stoushes, primarily centred in and around the Anglo-American academy. In fact, controversy erupted within Britain before the 2004 PACBI. Why? As Jewish academic Ronnie Fraser has written, Britain was more hospitable to BDS than elsewhere:

> First, academics are more organized there than in the United States or Western Europe and the labor unions allow [small coteries of] activists, many of them left-wing, to decide policies. More generally, labor unions have traditionally been powerful in Britain. Other reasons include the identification of Israel with Britain's colonial past and Britain's long association with the Middle East; the Balfour Declaration; [and]

leftist support for the Palestinians, which began during the 1960s and was complete by the time of the Lebanon War in 1982.

By contrast, in Fraser's opinion, French scholars are generally more cautious about taking anti-Israel actions that can be 'interpreted as anti-Semitic'; in the United States, the liberal Jewish community is better organised and finds that unions are more sympathetic to Israel's cause.[1]

So it was that in April 2002, British radical science academics Steven and Hilary Rose, 'initiated' a call for a moratorium on European research collaboration with Israeli academics and their higher education institutions in the form of an open letter co-signed by 123 academics published by the *Guardian* newspaper.[2] Using Israel's invasion of the West Bank cities as their professed rationale but ignoring the precipitating Palestinian violence and the complex causality behind the events of the Second Intifada, the Roses argued that a boycott was the only effective means of putting pressure on Israel to withdraw from the Occupied Territories and accept a two-state solution.[3] The resultant petition garnered 270 signatures from European Union scholars and from 10 anti-Zionist Israelis including Ilan Pappe and Tanya Reinhart.[4]

A successful motion was also passed at the Paris 6 University urging the European Union not to renew its preferential 1995 Association Agreement with Israel, but was later dropped after public outrage.

Boycott proposals led by churches and other non-government groups, including some British trade unions, emerged but mostly sank without trace. Campaigns were launched across 50 US universities, including Harvard and MIT, calling for the divestment of holdings in Israeli hi-tech company shares.[5] Unofficial and private boycotts of Israeli academics occurred including the exclusion of a scholarly article submitted by Oren Yiftachel, a professor at Ben-Gurion University, to the journal *Political Geography*.[6] Such tactics largely floundered against an outraged academy in Britain and elsewhere; however they spoke volumes of the original sin into which the BDS movement was born.

Matters took an ugly turn in May 2003. Mona Baker, an Egyptian-born translation studies scholar at the University of Manchester Institute of Science and Technology and co-signatory to the *Guardian* letter, acted upon the Rose's boycott proposal. Baker unilaterally blackbanned two Israeli academics from the editorial boards of two of her journals, *The Translator: Studies in Intercultural Communication*, and *Translation Studies Abstracts* on account of their connections to Israeli universities. Ironically, both of the boycotted academics had distinguished records as campaigners against Israeli human rights abuses – Bar-Ilan University's Miriam Shlesinger was a former chair of the Israeli branch of Amnesty International and a long-time activist with *Peace Now* – and along with the other sacked left-wing academic Gideon Toury of Tel Aviv

University, she was also a noted critic of the Sharon Likud government.[7]

Baker was widely criticised in the mainstream press and academic circles, including by the British National Union of Students. Led by Labour Prime Minister Tony Blair, the House of Commons condemned her 'downright anti-Semitic' 'discrimination'.[8] Pouring fuel on the fire in response, Baker claimed that 'the Jewish press in Britain is shamelessly and exclusively pro-Israel'.[9] Then, a few months later, writing with an American scholar Lawrence Davidson, she mounted an argument that smacked of classical anti-Semitism. Israeli universities should be singled out for sanctions, the authors wrote, 'because Zionist influence spreads far beyond its own immediate area of dominion, and now widely influences many key domestic agendas in the west'. 'Unlike the Chinese, Russians and other oppressive regimes ... the Israelis and their supporters directly influence the policy-makers of our own countries.'[10]

In the same year, Oxford University Professor Andrew Wilkie rejected the application of an Israeli to study for a PhD under his supervision. His stated reason was that the applicant had served in the Israeli Defence Forces (IDF).[11] Yet it was soon revealed that Wilkie had targeted for boycott an individual with no affiliation to an Israeli academic institution; indeed, his gravest sin was simply holding Israeli citizenship, which compels one to serve with the IDF. Moreover, the intimation that ex-IDF soldiers were automatically targets of a boycott effectively meant that a racist boycott of all Israeli Jews was henceforth morally justified; a crude form of collective punishment and ethnic stereotyping that would hallmark later BDS activities. Wilkie subsequently apologised. However, following his suspension by the University for a period of two months without pay, and resignation from several institutional positions, Wilkie received the support of the nascent boycott movement. Steven Rose described the University's disciplinary actions as a 'wholly disproportionate punishment'.[12] Other manifestations of the initial campaign included attempts to prevent Israeli academics from obtaining grants and campaigns to persuade universities to cut ties with Israeli institutions. In March 2004, more than 300 academics from around the world signed a petition calling on leaders of Israeli universities to reveal whether or not they supported current government policies towards the Palestinians.[13] These early boycott proposals met with limited success: there was some evidence of academics cancelling proposed joint projects with Israeli colleagues, refusing requests for research co-operation, and refusing to attend conferences in Israel, although the latter may have also reflected security rather than political concerns. The full extent of such activities is difficult to judge given that much of it may be concealed. On the other hand, no major academic institution or organisation endorsed the academic boycott, no American university voted to divest Israeli shares, the Paris University was forced by public protests to retract its motion, and a much greater number of academics internationally signed anti-boycott rather than pro-boycott petitions. Harvard University President Lawrence Summers publicly condemned the boycott as did the editors of the leading general science magazines, *Science* and *Nature*.[14]

In response to these embarrassments, the boycott campaign sought a 'more sophisticated formulation' that did not explicitly target individuals for simply being Israeli. Thus the concept of an 'institutional boycott' was born.[15] This tactic was soon put to the test, again in Britain, yet it stumbled at the first hurdle. In April 2003, upon a motion moved by pro-Palestinian University of Birmingham academic, Sue Blackwell, the 48000-member British Association of University Teachers (AUT) Council, one of Britain's then two official tertiary sector unions (representing 'older' institutions), voted by a two-to-one margin to reject boycotting Israel. The previous year AUT and the 69000-member National Association of Teachers in Further and Higher Education (NATFHE, the UK's second tertiary sector union, representing 'newer' institutions) had endorsed giving 'consideration' to just such a motion. Later that year, a conference was hosted by the London University School of Oriental and African Studies entitled 'Resisting Israeli Apartheid: Strategies and Principles', launching the British Committee for the Universities of Palestine (BRICUP).[16]

The boycott issue erupted on 22 April 2005 when Blackwell and her Birmingham colleague Shereen Benjamin moved another motion at the AUT's annual conference.[17] They argued that supporting a boycott responded to a 'clear call from Palestinians', namely the 2004 Palestinian Campaign for the Academic and Cultural Boycott of Israel (PACBI). Amid descriptions of Israel as a 'colonial', 'racist' entity practising 'apartheid' towards the Palestinians, on this occasion a motion to boycott and suspend activities with two Israeli universities, University of Haifa and Bar-Ilan University, passed by a narrow majority. In the former case, AUT Council argued that the boycott was initiated because the university had disciplined far-left Israeli historian Ilan Pappe over his supposed support of a student writing on the subject of the 1948 Arab-Israeli War. But these were only allegations that Pappe subsequently withdrew when sued for libel.[18] In the latter case, Council voted to boycott because Bar-Ilan helped to provide temporary degree programs at Ariel College in the West Bank.

As it happened, the motion's carriage was a travesty. No speeches against the motion were allowed, an unanticipated outcome of the executive committee's preferred option of opposing the motions by deferment of the motions (a tactic which only succeeded in regard to a third Israeli institution, Hebrew University). Further, the actual ballot was held late on a Friday prior to both the Jewish Sabbath and near to the significant festival of Pesach

(Passover), preventing many observant Jewish AUT members from voting. Additionally, anticipating the defeat of the relevant motions, Council voted to distribute pro-boycott literature to individual members, while a companion proposal to foster links between the union and Israeli counterparts was struck down. Significantly, in its so-called 'guidance' to members on these decisions, the AUT's executive committee mandated a non-compulsory boycott, albeit with the McCarthyist directive to members to consider exempting 'conscientious Israeli academics and intellectuals opposed to their state's colonial and racist policies'.[19]

International outrage quickly followed including calls for a counter boycott of AUT members. Others, led by left-wing scholars Jon Pike and David Hirsh, founded the online organisation 'Engage' to fight the boycott from within. More significantly, Haifa University and Hebrew University each began proceedings to sue AUT for libel. The latter institution also signed a joint statement with Al Quds University, an Arab University in Jerusalem, calling for academic co-operation between Israeli Jews and Arabs. Opposition was also expressed by several American academic associations, and 21 Nobel Prize laureates including Shimon Peres and Elie Wiesel. Even the generally anti-Israel *Guardian* opposed the boycott as 'McCarthyist' and 'counterproductive'; the more conservative *The Times* called the proposal 'a mockery of academic freedom', which represented 'an echo of the Nazi ban on Jewish academics'.

There was also almost universal opposition from the spectrum of Israeli and Jewish diaspora Left groups. However, the possibility that AUT and its individual members were in breach of UK equal opportunity and anti-discrimination legislation arguably dominated the subsequent reconsideration.

One month later, following a five-hour debate on 26 May 2005, AUT reversed its previous decision by a two-to-one margin. The union cited as its reason the potential damage inflicted upon notions of academic freedom and the hampering of dialogue and peace efforts between Israelis and Palestinians, remarkably insisting that boycotting Israel alone could not be justified.[20] It was strange that these reasons were not considered in the original decision. And the fact that Haifa University, a bastion of Jewish-Arab co-operation and reconciliation, or for that matter the other boycotted Israeli institutions, was not consulted in the initial decision process also raised troubling questions around due process and bias within AUT. Thus, not only had the affair inflicted considerable reputational damage upon the academic union, it was a severe setback to the boycott movement in general. And the rearguard action that secured the reversal probably prevented a domino effect in the academy. In one sense, BDS had suffered another ignominious setback. In another, the campaign had arrived on the global political agenda and come to the attention of thousands of previously unaware academics for the first time, even if for all the wrong reasons.

BDS supporters were unrepentant. The 'privileging of academic freedom as a super-value above all other freedoms is in principle antithetical to the very foundation of human rights', boycott leader Omar Barghouti and Palestinian-based academic Lisa Taraki wrote of the AUT reversal in a logically and morally inconsistent opinion piece. 'The right to live, and freedom from subjugation and colonial rule, to name a few, must be of more import than academic freedom. If the latter contributes in any way to suppression of the former, more fundamental rights, it must give way. By the same token, if the struggle to attain the former necessitates a level of restraint on the latter, then so be it.'[21] In other words, according to BDS activists of this ilk, there existed one rule for Israeli Jews and another for Palestinians and pro-boycott advocates.

A year later, the controversy re-erupted in June 2006, when NAFTHE passed a motion that criticised 'continuing Israeli apartheid policies, including construction of the exclusion wall, and discriminatory educational practices'. Then in classic McCarthyist terms, members were 'invited' 'to consider their own responsibility for ensuring equity and non-discrimination in contacts with Israeli educational institutions or individuals and to consider the appropriateness of a boycott of those that do not publicly dissociate themselves from such policies'.[22]

Although the motion passed, it ceased to be official policy two days later when the union merged with AUT to become the University and College

Union (UCU). The UCU passed a number of anti-Israel motions in June 2007 that explicitly favoured an academic boycott. In practice, the motions were not implemented because UCU received legal advice that they contravened British anti-discrimination legislation.[23] The centrepiece of BDS activism within academia had proved to be something of a disappointment. It would not however be the end of the story.

The success of the BDS in regard to unions outside academia was likewise limited in these years, despite triggers such as the 2006 Israeli-Hezbollah war. Peak bodies such as the American Federation of Labor and Congress of Industrial Organizations (AFL-CIO) shunned BDS. Somewhat later its President Richard L Sharka spoke out forcefully against the campaign.[24] No individual American trade union has endorsed BDS. By contrast, the Canadian union movement was somewhat more responsive. In 2006, the Ontario section of the Canadian Union of Public Employees (CUPE), which represents 200 000 workers, voted to join the boycott of Israel.[25] The move was heavily criticised at the time by Jewish communal leaders, politicians and opinion makers, but was overshadowed in January 2009 by the incendiary proposal of the CUPE Ontario University Workers Coordinating Committee to introduce a resolution that would ban Israeli academics from speaking, teaching or researching at Ontario universities. McCarthyism had reared its head again. 'Israeli academics should not be on our campuses', suggested CUPE Ontario President Sid Ryan, unless they 'explicitly condemn' Israeli policies.[26] His actions were denounced across the political spectrum, and also by Jewish groups, students, media outlets and academics.[27] CUPE National President Paul Moist criticised the plans and forced the committee to remove any reference to blacklisting Israeli academics.[28] One of the local CUPE branches publicly objected to the boycott initiative; some CUPE members wrote to Ryan demanding his resignation.[29] As it happened, the Ontario motion appears to have had very little practical effect. Few Canadian unions followed suit to actively support BDS and the Canadian Labour Congress, a three-million-strong umbrella organisation, has not endorsed BDS despite passing critical resolutions of Israel that nodded towards divestment from military works and boycotts of settlement goods.[30]

In Britain, the Trade Union Congress refused to formally back BDS despite supporting a prohibition against the importation of West Bank settlement products and voting to strengthen ties with the Palestine Solidarity Committee (PSC), arguably the main driver of BDS in Britain. In 2007, the British National Union of Journalists called for the boycotting of Israeli products, but failed to implement the resolution.[31] The Transport and General Workers Union passed boycott resolutions, as did Unison, Britain's largest public sector union with 1.3 million members. However, Unison's general secretary subsequently wrote to the Israeli Histadrut to say the motion was not really a boycott motion and urged the two organisations to continue to work together.[32] Also in 2007, the Irish Congress of Trade Unions backed divestment, a decision that was mirrored by IMPACT, the largest public-sector union in the Republic of Ireland, and the Northern Ireland Public Service Alliance. Somewhat earlier, in 2002, the Scottish Trades Union Congress (STUC) called for a temporary boycott of Israeli goods and services until Israel complied with certain UN resolutions. Its 2007 conference voted to explore BDS, but the next year decided to take no action because there had been no clear call for a boycott by the PGFTU.[33] In most cases, it was difficult to discern how these unions and peak bodies had actually moved to implement a boycott.

This fact points to a clear trend prior to 2009. The BDS movement boasted of numerous triumphs. Yet most pro-boycott decisions moved by unions were largely symbolic. BDS supporters also chose to highlight random actions by minor cultural organisations, companies, individuals and student organisations. In many instances these actors had clearly not signed onto the BDS cause in its entirety, or went so far as to deny that they had a pro-boycott policy.[34] The case of French transnational company Veolia (previously known as Connex, the company has been targeted over its involvement in building the East Jerusalem light-rail system) is a prime example. On several occasions when the transport and water management company was not offered a contract or its existing contract was not renewed, BDS activists claimed 'victory'. Mostly, BDS activists merely inferred the reasons behind each decision and more generally ignored the company's long-term strategy of withdrawing from the transport business.[35]

Formal BDS was also snubbed by mainstream religious organisations. Granted, major controversies broke out in 2004 when the General Assembly of the Presbyterian Church voted to 'initiate a process of phased selective divestment in multinational corporations operating in Israel'.[36] In 2005 the World Council of Churches condemned the occupation while highlighting its plans to apply 'economic pressure' to Israel.[37] Neither of these actions constituted support for formal BDS and in 2006 Presbyterians rescinded the 2004 decision. The relevant motion 'acknowledge[d] that [it] caused hurt and misunderstanding among many members of the Jewish community and within our Presbyterian communion'.[38] Nonetheless, these debates were accompanied by acrimonious public exchanges. It set a template for later BDS disputes, straining relationships between Jewish and Christian communities.

This trend was echoed in the experience of the small city of Somerville in the US state of Massachusetts. There a small activist group styling itself the Somerville Divestment Project (SDP) waged a two-year battle to convince the local municipality to divest from Israel. Initially the activists met with success when they managed to lobby the council to vote on a pro-divestment bill, the first of its kind in the United States. But before a final decision was taken the public was invited to comment, and in December 2004 the Somerville municipality rejected divestment. One reason for its defeat, aside from the mobilisation of local Jewish opposition, was the behaviour of pro-divestment activists. As American writer and pro-Israel activist John Haber writes, the 'yes' campaign 'cracked under the weight of its own fanaticism'; a frequent occurrence in BDS history. The group's tactics and public rhetoric became ever more extreme – despite its 'progressive' claims the SDP's website approvingly quoted anti-Israel figures from far-right American activist Pat Buchanan to the notorious Holocaust denialist and anti-Semite, Israel Shamir.[39]

Given the meagre harvest reaped in these years, perhaps the main function of the BDS campaign at this time was the performance of 'agit-prop' in the manner of crude protests and incendiary annual events such as 'Israeli Apartheid Week' held in February on North American and British campuses. And yet, despite the campaign's lack of objective successes, and for all the damage it has inflicted on a range of progressive organisations and local communities, the potential for a revived round of BDS activities endures as long as the Israeli-Palestinian conflict continues.

BDS in the wake of
Operation Cast Lead

The commencement of the Gaza War hostilities between Israel and the Islamic fundamentalist group Hamas during late 2008 and early 2009, a conflict known in the former as 'Operation Cast Lead', provided a new stimulus to BDS activities. As the civilian death toll and casualties rose to well over 1000, anti-Israel demonstrations were staged across the West. Inexorably, they were accompanied by renewed calls by pro-Palestinian activists for universities, unions, private companies, governments and individuals to observe the commandments of the BDS movement. A similar trend was evinced after the 2010 Freedom Flotilla controversy, in which IDF troops killed several (mostly Turkish) activists aboard a vessel intent on sailing to Gaza.

In the immediate aftermath of these events BDS claimed a handful of victories. In February 2009, Cardiff University, a minor British academic institution, voted to divest from BAE Systems owing to the company's arms manufacturing links with the IDF.[40] In April, a rather more influential body, the STUC did in fact vote to support BDS. Though renowned for its militancy this was the first peak union body in the world to show such explicit support.[41] Later in the year, the congress deputy secretary-general publicly urged supporters of the Glasgow Celtic football club to wave Palestinian flags at a home match against Israeli team Hapoel Tel Aviv in 'solidarity with suffering Palestinians', a call that was widely condemned including by the Celtic Football Club.[42] In October 2009, the University of Sussex Students' Union became the first such organisation in Britain to vote for a boycott of Israeli goods.[43]

In the United States, in February 2009, the small private liberal arts Hampshire College in Western Massachusetts ostensibly bowed to pressure by the notorious BDS lobby group, Students for Justice in Palestine (SJP) to divest its (small) endowment fund from companies allegedly profiting from the occupation, including Motorola, Caterpillar and General Electric. BDS activists hailed a totemic victory given Hampshire's pioneering divest from South Africa in the 1980s.[44] But the College's board of trustees denied that they had divested from Israel and trumpeted their continuing desire to invest in Israeli firms, triggering a flurry of angry denunciations from BDS advocates.[45] (The official BDS website still claims Hampshire as a successful example of divestment).[46] Far from constituting some kind of Waterloo, these cases proved the exception to the rule.

After the Gaza War, some success was achieved within Western-based Christian groups. In 2009, the World Council of Churches adopted an anti-Israel divestment resolution and the next year formally called for a boycott of products originating from West Bank settlements. In June 2010, the

British Methodist Church followed suit, becoming the first major Christian denomination in Britain to officially adopt such a policy. These decisions aroused the ire of Jewish communal groups, but in reality neither body was signing up to the extreme demands of the BDS movement.[47]

Once again, the major forum of BDS controversy was the UK's University and College Union.[48] At its 2009 annual conference, the union passed a resolution to boycott Israeli academics and universities by a large majority. The relevant motion argued that all Israeli academics were complicit in their government's policy towards Palestinians. However, the vote was immediately declared invalid as legal advice repeated previous warnings that such a boycott would likely trigger legal action against the union and its individual members under Britain's racial discrimination laws.

More worryingly, during the voting process prominent UCU members were actively involved in distributing anti-Semitic material alleging that Jewish financial and political power underpinned opposition to the boycott motion. UCU activist Jenna Delich openly circulated an anti-Jewish conspiracy theory from David Duke's far-right website to hundreds of UCU members on its activist list. Further, a senior UCU official Mike Cushman publicly argued that the British Labour Government was controlled by Zionist finance, and the University College of London UCU Branch Secretary Sean Wallis suggested that opponents of the BDS were bankrolled by the notorious Lehman Brothers investment bank. None of these anti-Jewish activities were repudiated by UCU.[49]

The UCU also invited an unrepentant anti-Semite, South African trade unionist Bongani Masuku – whose threats in March 2009 against Jewish businesses and supporters of Israel declaring that they must leave the country were condemned as hate speech by the South African Human Rights Commission – to address a UCU forum in favour of BDS.[50] These anti-Jewish actions led to the mass resignations of approximately 300 Jewish members from the union.[51] Additionally, a Jewish member of the UCU, Ronnie Fraser, took the union to an Employment Tribunal for allegedly breaching the Equality Act 2010 by creating a hostile and discriminatory environment. Fraser's legal action was unsuccessful, but nevertheless exposed systemic anti-Semitism within UCU.[52]

Overall, the UCU and STUC examples cut across the grain of the continuing inability of BDS activities to secure union support. While British unions were susceptible to boycott calls, the exceptionally pro-Israel American labour movement remained hostile. Crucially, at its June 2010 second world congress the International Trade Union Confederation (ITUC) representing 312 affiliated organisations in 156 countries and territories and 176 million workers rejected calls to support BDS, including an incendiary South African motion. Rubbing salt into the wounds, the Histadrut's leader,

Ofer Eini, was elevated to the ITUC's 25-member Executive Board as well as its General Council as a Vice President. In fact, a resolution adopted by the ITUC congress congratulated the co-opera- tive work between Histadrut and the PGFTU on the rights of Palestinian workers. While critical of many Israeli policies, calling for an end to illegal settlements in the Palestinian territories, rejecting the blockade of Gaza and the building of a security fence, the congress explicitly rejected 'the extremist policies of Hamas'.[53]

Consumer-led boycotts gave some impe- tus to the BDS movement. Following Operation Cast Lead, the US-based feminist-activist group CodePink launched a 'Stolen Beauty' campaign against the Israeli cosmetic company Ahava. The company, according to its critics, is located on the Palestinian side of the Green Line and not only mis- leadingly labels its products as Israeli in origin but profits from the occupation because its products are made from Dead Sea mud sourced from the set- tlement and kibbutz Mitzpe Shalem. The CodePink activists engaged in social media and in-store pro- tests such as rowdy 'bikini brigades' of female activ- ists covered in mud aimed at retailers who stocked Ahava products. CodePink activists point to a seem- ing upsurge in public awareness of the Palestinians' plight. However, their major victory appears to have been the successful pressure applied to the Oxfam charity to suspend American actress Kristen Davis as a Goodwill Ambassador due to her spokesperson role with the Israeli cosmetics company Ahava Sea Laboratories, and the 'closure' of the Ahava store in London's Covent Gardens (in fact the landlord decided not to renew the lease because of complaints from neighbouring businesses).[54]

One particularly contentious post-2009 case involved the small Olympia food co-op store in the State of Washington in the United States. In July 2010 Olympia decided to stop selling all products originating from Israel, and not merely settlement produce, in its two grocery stores. The stores were uniquely susceptible to an emotion-based campaign as they were based in the hometown of Rachel Corrie, a 23-year-old pro-Palestinian activist working with the extremist International Solidarity Movement when she was struck and killed by an Israeli bulldozer in Gaza at the height of the Second Intifada in 2003. The boycott push was championed from 2008 onwards by the local chapter of the BDS movement who explicitly identified with the goals of the BDS movement. However, the opinions of the co-op staff were divided so the board was called in to make a final deliberation. On July 15, the 10-member co-op board voted 9–0 with one abstention to boycott Israeli products as a way to 'compel Israel to follow international law and respect Palestinian human rights'. The hasty decision by the board to support BDS was allegedly made under duress of some 40 to 50 BDS activists, with no space granted to dissenting voices and without any recourse to the co-op's membership, a classic cadre-like tactic of many BDS activists. As a result of the co-op's boycott, gluten-free crackers, ice-cream cones and a moisturising cream were removed from sale.[55] It hardly seemed worth the tumult and shouting that subsequently embroiled the co-op.

To its credit, the co-op had a pre-existing boycott policy that had been deployed to protest Norwegian whaling and China's human-rights record. Nonetheless, the anti-Israeli decision subsequently made international headlines and outraged Jewish members, who accused the co-op of bad faith negotiating vis-à-vis the boycott vote.[56] Accusations of anti-Semitism emerged. This much was admitted by the co-op board: 'Unfortunately, anti-Semitic statements have abounded in a lot of the "support" that the co-op has received in regard to the Israeli-products' boycott.'[57] The decision was subsequently opened up for discussion among the co-op's members, but the board's decision was upheld. Despite a costly legal challenge, and further protests from the local Jewish community backed by outside lobby groups, the boycott remains in place.[58]

A similarly divisive if ultimately unsuccessful American BDS campaign took place across 2012 at Park Slope Food Co-op, a liberal and Jewish bastion in New York's Brooklyn district. On this occasion the motion favouring a boycott was subjected to full scrutiny and the debate raged for many months. Despite the store selling only a handful of Israeli-made products, the debate divided the co-op's 15 000 members – a physical fight broke out between proponents at one point. Local politicians weighed in against BDS.[59] Arguably the comfortable 'no' vote paled in comparison with the national and international exposure the Park Slope example garnered for the BDS movement, allowing an extremist interpretation of the Israel-Palestine conflict to be widely broadcast. Indeed this increasingly seemed to be the very purpose of BDS campaigns.

Given the lack of institutional support, one successful tactic of BDS supporters was to play up a relatively small number of celebrity endorsements. For the most part this consisted of artists and musicians turning down invitations to visit Israel or well-known anti-Israeli activists reiterating previous declarations of BDS support. Following the 2008–09 Gaza war for example, Jewish Canadian left-wing activist and writer Naomi Klein endorsed the campaign in two newspaper columns as if her views on the conflict were already not well-known.[60] Conversely, the overwhelming majority of artists, actors, writers and public intellectuals either take no interest in BDS or in some cases have explicitly denounced the campaign, such as English novelist Ian McEwan amid controversy surrounding his 2011 Jerusalem Prize award.[61] Perhaps the most celebrated BDS 'recruit' is the world-renowned theoretical physicist, Englishman Stephen Hawking, who in mid-2013 ostensibly came out in support of an academic boycott of Israel after withdrawing from the President's Conference held by Israeli head of state and former politician Shimon Peres. Touted as a great victory, in fact Hawking's decision underlined the hypocrisy of BDS (and he did not endorse the blanket boycott campaign). Hawking is a paraplegic who communicates via a sophisticated computer device, largely designed and manufactured in Israel. If Hawking were to truly boycott Israel he would literally cease to function intellectually and in everyday life.

Overall, between 2009 and 2012, few individuals, companies and civil society groupings in Britain and North America signed up to BDS. Why? Arguably, most saw through the tactic of waging warfare against Israel by means other than violence. Another crucial stumbling block was the refusal of the Palestinian Authority (or even Hamas technically) to officially support BDS. Rather the PA, in its own words, supports 'a boycott only against products made in West Bank settlements'. 'We are neighbors with Israel, we have agreements with Israel, we recognize Israel, we are not asking anyone to boycott products of Israel', Majdi Khaldi, an adviser to Palestinian Authority leader Mahmoud Abbas remarked when pointing out that the Palestinian leadership did not support the blanket boycott of Israel. These were sentiments echoed by Abbas himself.[62] Whether principled or pragmatic, this position reflects the Palestinian Authority's basic acceptance of Israel's right to exist, and that Palestinian businesses and universities co-operate with the Israeli government, civil society and private companies on a daily basis. A blanket boycott would prove catastrophic for the Palestinian economy and ordinary workers. A similar logic is used by many Palestinian academics, including Sari Nusseibeh, president of Al-Quds University, who opposes a boycott of Israeli universities.[63] Granted, these inconvenient examples of opposition count for little in the eyes of BDS militants. The PA and Fatah (the secular nationalist Palestinian political party which essentially controls the West Bank) are regarded by such activists as 'traitors' to the Palestinian cause.[64]

Criticisms by leading anti-Zionist, pro-Palestinian Jewish academics Noam Chomsky and Norman Finkelstein have played a part. Chomsky, who says that he technically supports BDS, argues that a general boycott is 'a gift to Israeli hardliners and their American supporters' and can only harm the Palestinian movement. The BDS of 'one man NGOs' was not supported by the Palestinians and reeked of 'hypocrisy'; 'why not boycott the United States? ... Israeli crimes [are] a fragment of US crimes'. He also recently criticised the demands for a Right of Return and the frequent analogies made with South African Apartheid.[65] Likewise, Finkelstein believes that unless the BDS movement explicitly includes as a 'goal' the 'recognition of Israel' its message 'won't reach the public'. He regards the current BDS movement as a 'hypocritical, dishonest cult' led by 'dishonest gurus' prone to exaggerate their successes; they 'cleverly pose as human rights activists', but ultimately desire 'the destruction of Israel.'[66]

That high-profile Jewish pro-Palestinians are critics or completely opposed to the BDS campaign bodes ill indeed. Above all, BDS activists appear expert at kicking own goals. Protests such as that carried out by the aggressive British-based Palestine Solidarity Committee at a performance by the Israel Philharmonic Orchestra at London's Royal Albert Hall in February 2011 gave off the appearance of crude racism.[67] Little wonder that BDS struggles to win mainstream support.

Impact of the Gaza Wars

For all its foibles, BDS has been kept alive by the failure of Israel and the Palestinian Authority to strike a two-state agreement and repeated outbreaks of violence between Israel and Hamas. There is some evidence that the long-run campaign waged by BDS activists within unions and the academy is paying off. Perhaps the most significant example was the July 2014 decision of Britain's largest union Unite to formally support BDS.[68]

BDS finally broke through in America post-April 2013 when a number of small scholarly organisations voted to support BDS. Their ranks have included the Association for Asian American Studies, the Native American and Indigenous Studies Association, the Critical Ethnic Studies Association, the Peace and Justice Studies Association, the Middle East Studies Association, the African Literature Association and the American Studies Association (ASA). The most high-profile case involved the December 2013 decision of the National Council of ASA to boycott Israeli universities, a decision later ratified by the association's 5000 members. ASA's president Curtis Marez argued that America has 'a particular responsibility to answer the call for boycott because it is the largest supplier of military aid to the state of Israel', which begged the question as to why the association didn't boycott the United States or refuse to accept government funding.

The move provoked a storm of protest from Jewish groups in the United States. The ASA motion was widely condemned by members of the US House of Representatives as well as New York State assemblymen. More than 200 American colleges and universities and academic umbrella organisations such as the 48 000-member American Association of University Professors and the Association of American Universities publicly denounced the decision, as did the Executive Committee of the Association of American Universities, which represents 62 leading institutions in North America.[69] In any case, the implications of this 'victory' should be qualified. The ASA vote amounted to 1252 members or a quarter of its membership. The resolution permitted members to continue to collaborate with individual Israelis.[70] Moreover, the resolution was largely symbolic. The ASA has rarely entered into partnerships with Israeli institutions and the overwhelming majority of academic bodies in the United States reject BDS.

BDS gains among British academia and student politics also remain limited. In April 2013, the 14 500-member Teachers' Union of Ireland became the first lecturers' association in Europe to call for an academic boycott of Israel.[71] The National Union of Teachers, which has more than 300 000 members in England and Wales, making it the largest union of its type in Europe, passed a resolution backing a boycott of companies profiting from Israel's settlements in the West Bank. Contrary to the claim of pro-Palestinian 'freelance' journalist Ben White this decision did not constitute a full, blanket BDS-style boycott.[72] In 2014, Ireland's National University of Ireland (Galway) Students' Union passed a pro-BDS motion. More significantly, in August 2014, Britain's National Union of Students (NUS) ostensibly voted to adopt BDS. In fact the relevant motion merely amended the union's policy, allowing student unions across the United Kingdom to theoretically 'impose sanctions on Israel and support campaigns to boycott Israeli products on campuses'.[73]

The NUS, as an umbrella organisation does not possess the power to issue a binding directive to affiliates. This symbolic statement was arguably overshadowed by the rejections of groupings like the Oxford University Students' Union in March 2013. And yet, in its defeat, this example revealed the dark underbelly of BDS activism. The week of voting at Oxford was marred by hate mail, accusations of racism, and the spectacular walkout from a debate by former Labour and far-left Respect Party

MP George Galloway who declared: 'I refused this evening to debate with an Israeli, a supporter of the Apartheid state of Israel. The reason is simple: No recognition, No normalization. Just Boycott, divestment and sanctions, until the Apartheid state is defeated.' Galloway provoked a national uproar the next year when he declared that his constituency of Bradford was an 'Israeli free zone' prompting a police investigation.[74]

In the United States, a handful of student bodies have passed divestment motions. Most significant are the two University of California Berkeley resolutions of 2010 and 2013 that garnered international attention. In March 2010, the leaders of Berkeley's Student Senate voted 16–4 in favour of bill number 118 entitled 'In Support of ASUC Divestment from War Crimes'. The bill specifically sought to pressure the University to divest from two US companies whose products were allegedly used in the 2006 Lebanon War between Israel and Hezbollah and 2008 Operation Cast Lead. While the decision was of symbolic value it brought no economic pressure to bear upon Israel as the targets were actually American companies – General Electric and United Technologies – and the divisive debate that accompanied the vote rent the campus in two. Moreover, the motion was subsequently vetoed by the student union president Will Smelko, who claimed that the decision constituted 'a symbolic attack on a specific community' and had been passed with indecent haste. The open hearings that followed that decision featured all-night meetings, the interventions of Nobel laureates, university professors and government officials. The first debate featured an anti-Semitic cry from one BDS supporter: 'you killed Jesus'. The vote to overturn the veto failed by 13–5–1, but arguably the BDS case had been given an international publicity boost.[75] In 2013, however, a motion was passed on the University of California's San Diego campus which was not vetoed by the incumbent president Connor Landgraf even though he heavily criticised the bill's 'one-sided narrative' and 'utter failure to create any constructive discussion or dialogue'; it 'served to do nothing more than divide our campus, foster anger, and encourage divisiveness'. He explicitly decried any link between the motion and BDS: 'it cannot and should not take this as a victory'.[76] Across 2012–13 divestment bills passed on two other University of California campuses, Riverside and Irvine.[77]

For all the heat of the BDS debates, the academy is not the main game. Owing to the hostility of its neighbours, Israel is reliant on trade with Western Europe, North America and countries such as Australia. Of more concern are examples of Northern European companies and government bodies divesting from Israeli companies who do business in West Bank settlements, even if this scarcely represents a vindication of the formal BDS campaign.[78] Smaller-scale consumer boycotts are likely to grow in number,[79] along with a renewed focus on celebrity endorsements. The leading actress Scarlett Johansson resisted pressure from Oxfam International with whom she had been associated as Global Ambassador, and reaffirmed her promotional role with the Israeli company SodaStream even though one of its factories was based in the West Bank settlement of Ma'ale Adumim.[80] However in late October 2014 SodaStream announced that it was shutting the aforementioned factory, a move interpreted by many as owing to BDS activism. Yet, a number of leading musicians have performed in Israel during 2014 including the Rolling Stones, Justin Timberlake, Alicia Keys, Cyndi Lauper, Deep Purple and Lady Gaga (Neil Young cancelled his shows citing security concerns).[81]

Finally, some liberal churches in North America have recently undertaken some boycott initiatives. In 2012, the United Church of Canada, the largest Christian denomination in the country, started a campaign to boycott products made in the settlements.[82] In June 2014, the 2.4-million member Presbyterian Church of the United States voted to divest itself of Israeli shareholdings in three multinational companies long targeted by BDS activists: Caterpillar, Hewlett-Packard and Motorola Solutions.[83] The decision aroused much anger within the American Jewish community, but should be taken with a grain of salt. The Church has previously rejected calls for a 'blanket divestment' of Israel before reversing course.

How do we explain the recent spike in BDS support and, more commonly, anti-settlement divestments? The scenes of carnage and death arising out of the Gaza Wars of 2012 and 2014 have produced a visceral effect across the West, feeding the notion that Israel is a Goliath oppressing the Palestinian David. Undoubtedly the continued rightwards drift of Israeli politics has contributed to a willingness of business and other organisations to distance themselves from the practices of Binyamin Netanyahu's government, which includes the instalment in leading positions of pro-settler politicians such as Avigdor Lieberman and Naftali Bennett. In a similar vein, anti-BDS moves from within Israel have arguably proved counterproductive. For instance, in 2011, the Israeli Knesset passed a widely criticised law making a boycott call by an Israeli individual or organisation a civil offence, which can potentially result in a fine or removal of state assistance. In the wake of the 2014 July–August Gaza conflict Israel seemingly faces a renewed campaign of international isolation, albeit one largely limited to targeting Israeli economic activity in the West Bank settlements and foreign-owned entities. And this is to say nothing of the phenomenon of concealed boycotts, whereby Israeli businesses, artists and academics face an increasing refusal of international agencies and potential partners to collaborate with them, due to the political baggage the conflict brings with it.

Overall, the formal BDS campaign has failed to attract the support of key Western interests. Private companies, governments, academics and civil society organisations have for the most part gone out of their way not to endorse BDS. Why? BDS activists appear to have learnt little from early controversies. In 2014, at least two pro-BDS ballots within American student unions and associated bodies were scheduled for Shabbat and Passover.[84] Such campaigns to exclude Jewish voters are scarcely likely to attract the kind of mainstream support the movement craves. Public outrage followed the decision by a London branch of the Sainsbury's supermarket chain to remove all Kosher (Israeli or not) products from its shelves in the face of aggressive in-store behaviour by BDS supporters.[85] Shortly afterwards, a British security guard refused Jewish school children entry to a sporting goods store informing them: *'no Jews, no Jews'*.[86]

Yet BDS proponents continue to trumpet their inexorable triumph, endlessly proclaiming the latest 'tipping point'. In reality, BDS has left a trail of acrimonious debates, in part encouraged by the mainstreaming of anti-Semitic public discourse within the West, and pushed diaspora Jews away from progressively minded organisations. That these goings-on are considered to be victories of a kind speaks more to the delusion and moral vanity of BDS activists than any substantive achievement.

Conclusion:
The progressive alternative
to BDS

During the latter stages of our writing of this book the wrong-headed logic of the BDS movement was vividly illustrated. As a direct result of the American Studies Association's 2013 decision to implement a boycott of Israeli universities, the academic supervisor of a doctoral student enrolled at Tel Aviv University was unable to enlist qualified examiners to review his student's thesis. To BDS activists this constitutes a success. But for the student in question – a Palestinian-Arab citizen of Israel – it was surely a personal tragedy. That in 2012 the targeted university's president, Joseph Klafter, had courageously granted approval to student organisations seeking to hold demonstrations on campus commemorating the Nakba, earning him a nationalist-inspired backlash, only added to the cruel sense of farce.[1]

Aside from its disastrous effect upon innocent individuals and institutions, this example also serves to demonstrate why BDS is the antithesis of what is required to progress the cause of peace between the Palestinians and Israelis. A progressive path to

peace will ultimately be based upon three principles: empathy, dialogue and compromise. Here
of course was an example of an Israeli institution
publicly recognising that empathy for, or at the very
least public discussion of, the Palestinian narrative,
of which the Nakba plays a central role, is key to
maintaining dialogue between the two peoples and,
ultimately, the kind of mutual compromise that will
lead to long-term coexistence in the form of two
states.

'Israel exists; the Palestinian people exist. Neither is provisional', David Remnick, editor of the
New Yorker recently wrote. 'Within these territorial
confines, two nationally distinct groups, who are
divided by language, culture, and history, cannot
live wholly apart or wholly together.'[2] This is the
messy basis upon which two states must be built.
We do not pretend to have all the answers to solving
this bitter and complex conflict. We are at present
highly pessimistic about the chances of a peace deal
being struck in the near future. We are also realistic
about our own ability to progress that outcome. The
Jewish diaspora, Australians and any Westerners for
that matter, will not be able to impose peace upon
the combatants. Agency ultimately rests with the
two peoples in question, on the ground in Israel and
the Palestinian territories, not on a distant university campus. This is not to suggest that some form
of international intervention such as a trusteeship
over the West Bank will not be necessary to break
the deadlock required to guarantee Israeli security

needs and genuine Palestinian self-determination.[3] Rather, a sense of humility on the part of outsiders is necessary. Practical support rather than empty sloganeering is required. Helping each side of the conflict talk with each other rather than boycott one another is a pretty good place to start. It is therefore high time that BDS activists who claim to support the Palestinian yearning for national independence were sent a clear message: get out of the way of those people who are genuinely committed to fostering the preconditions of a two-state solution.

So how can progressives and all people of goodwill best assist the peace process? We suggest that there a number of alternative strategies to a BDS to achieve a two-state solution which conform to our guiding principles: empathy, dialogue and compromise. As a start, the Geneva Peace Accord negotiated by a team of prominent Israeli and Palestinian negotiators in 2003, despite being non-binding, remains the benchmark for Israeli-Palestinian conflict resolution.[4] The Accord, which proposed the establishment of a demilitarised Palestinian State in the West Bank and Gaza Strip alongside Israel accompanied by minor land swaps, was rejected by hardliners on both sides, but attracted significant support from ordinary Israelis and Palestinians.[5] Its key principles of mutual recognition and compromise have since been progressed by the Geneva Initiative, an ongoing campaign to promote a negotiated two-state solution. This is stridently opposed by the BDS movement.[6]

Other valuable Israeli–Palestinian peace initiatives exist at the grassroots level. One such initiative is the Parents Circle – Families Forum, which includes about 600 Israeli and Palestinian families who have lost relatives to violence associated with the conflict. The Forum enables members to recognise the other side's suffering, and channel their personal grief into constructive activities for peace and reconciliation rather than ongoing violence and revenge. Another initiative is the OneVoice Movement, which hosts a number of public forums and activities aimed at jointly promoting Israeli and Palestinian support for peace. Trade Unions Linking Israel and Palestine (TULIP) is an international organisation that promotes co-operation between Israeli and Palestinian trade unions, with the overarching aim of promoting the viability of a two-state solution. Additionally, there is the Peres Center for Peace, a non-political organisation that promotes partnerships between Israelis and Palestinians in a range of health, cultural and sporting areas.[7]

A more recent peace venture involved the establishment of a pro-peace, anti-academic-boycott network by a group of progressive scholars in the United States. The network, which has called itself the Third Narrative Academic Advisory Council, rejects black-and-white interpretations of the conflict. Instead, the Council emphasises the importance of 'empathy for the suffering and aspirations of both peoples and respect for their national narratives'. The Council asserts that critical and open

academic analysis and dialogue is essential for progressing a peaceful two-state solution.[8]

What is common to all these activities is a belief
that there is no simplistic right and wrong in the
Israeli-Palestinian conflict. Rather, both sides have
legitimate claims to national self-determination and
statehood. Mutual recognition of the validity of
both narratives is required to advance negotiations
that result in two states for two peoples. We out-
line in Appendix 2 how moderate pro-Palestinians
and moderate pro-Israelis can find common ground
around this two-state scenario. In contrast, as we
also note in Appendix 2, extremists from both sides
of the divide, whether Greater Israel supporters or
BDS advocates, desperately want Israelis and Palestinians, their diaspora populations and other parties
to stop talking to each other in the ways that we
have outlined. What we are proposing in response
is serving them a dose of their own medicine: fostering more dialogue and collaboration, in other words
a boycott of the boycotters. Ironically, as we have
frequently seen in this book, that is not always the
easiest nor the most-favoured option. Yet the ability
to keep thinking and to keep talking in this intellectual equivalent of a no-man's-land might be the best
weapon that the true friends of peace possess.

Appendix 1

BDS myths and facts

- MYTH: The BDS is a non-violent political strategy that rejects the suicide bombings and other forms of terror previously utilised by Palestinians against Israeli civilians.
- FACT: The BDS does not involve a principled rejection of terrorism. Rather, it promotes boycott as a more effective means of waging political war against Israel.

- MYTH: The BDS is designed to protect the human rights of Palestinians. It is not intended to harm the rights of Israelis.
- FACT: If successful, the BDS would almost certainly produce the ethnic cleansing of most Israeli Jews from their homeland.

- MYTH: Opponents of BDS are right-wing Zionists who oppose Palestinian national rights.
- FACT: Many of the leading critics of BDS are two-staters who support the creation of a Palestinian State alongside Israel.

- MYTH: BDS supporters are moderates who merely wish to promote the same human rights for Palestinians that exist for Israelis.
- FACT: Most of the leading BDS advocates are long-time extremists who support the destruction of Israel and its replacement by an Arab majority state of Greater Palestine.

- MYTH: The BDS movement eschews all forms of racism including anti-Semitism.
- FACT: The BDS movement is based on the ethnic stereotyping of all Israelis and Jewish supporters of Israel as evil, and has produced numerous manifestations of anti-Semitism.

- MYTH: Jewish anti-Zionists who support BDS are a growing force in Jewish life internationally.
- FACT: Jewish anti-Zionists are a tiny group in Jewish communities, and would constitute well below one per cent of the Jewish population. They are even a small minority amongst left-wing Jews.

Appendix 2

One state or two?
A brief guide to solving the
Israeli–Palestinian conflict

Hardline Pro-Palestinian	Moderate Pro-Palestinian	Moderate Pro-Israel	Hardline Pro-Israel
Zero sum solution providing justice for Palestinians only – One State: Greater Palestine. Demands that Israeli Jews surrender, and give up statehood.	Win-win solution providing partial justice for both sides – Two States: Palestine and Israel. This perspective is critical of key assumptions of Zionism, but still believes Israeli Jews have a right to statehood.	Win-win solution providing partial justice for both sides – Two States: Israel and Palestine. This perspective is critical of key aspects of Palestinian political culture, but still believes they are entitled to a state.	Zero sum solution providing justice for Israelis only – One State: Greater Israel. Demands that Palestinians surrender, and give up claims to statehood.
Abolish Israel by violent or other means.	Accept Israel's existence within Green Line borders.	Support creation of Palestinian State in West Bank and Gaza Strip alongside Israel.	Support territorial expansion of Israel to include most or whole of West Bank.

Hardline Pro-Palestinian	Moderate Pro-Palestinian	Moderate Pro-Israel	Hardline Pro-Israel
Create Palestine in place of Israel.	Create independent and contiguous Palestinian State alongside Israel.	Create Palestinian State alongside Israel.	Oppose Palestinian State
Demand coerced return of millions of 1948 Palestinian refugees to Green Line Israel.	Accept that most if not all refugees requesting to return will need to be resettled within Palestinian State.	Recognise Palestinian suffering in 1948 War, but reject any return of refugees to Green Line Israel.	Oppose any recognition of Palestinian refugee rights.
Demand that Palestinian Arabs living within Green Line Israel be recognised as a national community and component of larger Arab and Islamic nation.	Accept that Palestinian national claims will mainly be progressed within a Palestinian State, rather than within Israel.	Support full civil and political equality for all Arab citizens of Israel.	Oppose any recognition of political rights for Arabs living within Israel or the West Bank.

Notes

Introduction

1   'Israel: Greens NSW back international Boycotts, Divestment and Sanctions', NSW Greens Media Release, 7 December 2010, www.nsw.greens.org.au/content/israel-greens-nsw-back-international-boycotts-divestment-and-sanctions, accessed March 2014.

2   Mark Dodd and Sid Maher, 'Bob Brown told to rein in anti-Israel senator Lee Rhiannon', *The Australian*, 1 April 2011, www.theaustralian.com.au/national-affairs/bob-brown-told-to-rein-in-anti-israel-senator-lee-rhiannon/story-fn59niix-1226031644809?nk=b255cb5371bbbf4722b8f23f92ee48ae.

3   Philip Mendes, 'Israel's Camp David peace proposal: generous offer or sham?', *Australian Quarterly*, Vol. 76, no.1, January–February 2004, pp. 14–17.

4   Ahmed Moor, 'BDS is a long term project with radically transformative potential', *Mondoweiss*, 22 April 2010, www.mondoweiss.net/2010/04/bds-is-a-long-term-project-with-radically-transformative-potential.

5   Justin Huggler and Josie Ensor, 'Anti-Semitism on the march: Europe braces for violence', *The Telegraph* (London), 26 July 2014, www.telegraph.co.uk/news/worldnews/europe/10992886/Anti-Semitism-on-the-march-Europe-braces-for-violence.html, accessed July 2014.

6   Desmond Tutu (2003) 'Israel: time to divest', *New Internationalist*, no. 353, 2003, www.newint.org/columns/viewfrom/2003/01/01/israel/.

7   Author Unknown, 'Pig's head among kosher food in South African anti-Israel protest', *Haaretz*, 25 October 2014, www.haaretz.com/jewish-world/jewish-world-news/1.622673.

8   Peter Wertheim and Julie Nathan, 'The ugly face of student activism', *The Australian*, 30 April 2013, www.theaustralian.com.au/national-affairs/opinion/the-ugly-face-of-student-activism/story-e6frgd0x-1226631853245, accessed March 2014.

9   Kevin Rawlinson, 'George Galloway investigated by police for saying Bradford an "Israel-free zone"', *Guardian* (London), www.theguardian.com/politics/2014/aug/07/george-galloway-investigated-police-bradford-israel-free-zone, accessed August 2014.

10   See the founding statement of TULIP: www.tuliponline.org/?p=48, accessed March 2014.

11   'Paul Howes' address to the Zionist Federation of Australia Biennial', www.zfa.com.au/blog/2010/10/13/paul-howes-zfa-address/, accessed March 2014.

12   Dauod Kuttab, 'At Mandela funeral, Abbas says he opposes boycott of Israel', *Al Monitor*, 13 December 2013, www.al-monitor.com/pulse/originals/2013/12/abbas-attacks-bds. html.

13   Author Unknown, 'Palestinian university president comes out against boycott of Israeli academics', *Haaretz*, 17 June 2006, www. haaretz.com/news/palestinian-university-president-comes-out-against-boycott-of-israeli-academics-1.190585.

14   Audrea Lim (ed.), *The Case for Sanctions against Israel*, Verso, London, 2012, p. 3.

15   Maia Carter Hallward, *Transnational Activism and the Israeli-Palestinian Conflict*, Palgrave Macmillan, New York, 2013, p. 198.

16   Cary Nelson and Gabriel Noah Brahm, *The Case Against Academic Boycotts of Israel*, Wayne State University Press, Chicago, 2015. See also former United States Deputy Undersecretary of Defense Jed Babbin's right-wing account *The BDS War Against Israel* (2014).

17   Omar Barghouti, *Boycott, Divestment, Sanctions: The Global Struggle for Palestinian Rights*, Haymarket Books, Chicago, 2011; Manfred Gerstenfeld, *Academics against Israel and the Jews*, Jerusalem Center for Public Affairs, Jerusalem, 2007; Gershom Gorenberg, *The Unmaking of Israel*, HarperCollins, New York, 2011; Ari Shavit, *My Promised Land: the Triumph and Tragedy of Israel*, Scribe, Melbourne, 2014; Peter Beinart, *The Crisis of Zionism*, Henry Holt, New York, 2012.

1   The Left, Zionism and Israel, 1897–2014

1   Much of the argument in this chapter is drawn from Chapter 3 of Philip Mendes, *Jews and the Left: The rise and fall of a political alliance*, Palgrave Macmillan, London, 2014, and is reproduced here with the permission of Palgrave Macmillan.

2   Robert Wistrich, 'Marxism and Jewish Nationalism: The Theoretical Roots of Confrontation', in Robert Wistrich (ed.), *The Left Against Zion*, Valentine Mitchell, London, 1979.

3   J Stern, (1896–97) 'Review of T Herzl's book, *Der Judenstaat. Versuch einer modernen Losung der Judenfrage*, *Die Neue Zeit*, 15 (1), p. 186; Johann Pollak, 'Der politische Zionismus', *Die Neue Zeit*, vol. 16, no. 1, 1897–98, p. 600.

4   Jonathan Frankel, 'The Soviet regime and Anti-Zionism: An Analysis', in Ezra Mendelsohn (ed.), *Essential Papers on Jews and the Left*, New York University Press, New York, 1997.

5   Joshua M Karlip, *The tragedy of a generation: The rise and fall of Jewish nationalism in Eastern Europe*, Harvard University Press, Cambridge, 2013.

6   Yehuda Eloni, 'The Zionist Movement and the German Social Democratic Party, 1897–1918', *Studies in Zionism*, vol. 5, no. 2, 1984, pp. 192–93; Enzo Traverso, *The Marxists and the Jewish Question*, Humanities Press, New Jersey, 1994, p. 72.

7   Elias Heifetz, *The Slaughter of the Jews in the Ukraine in 1919*, Thomas Seltzer, New York, 1921.

8   Jacob Hen-Tov, *The Comintern and Zionism in Palestine*, PhD thesis, Brandeis University, 1969.

9   Marc Jarblum, *The Socialist International and Zionism*, Poale Zion of America, New York, 1933.

10   Christine Collette, 'The utopian visions of Labour Zionism, British Labour, and the Labour and Socialist International in the 1930s', in Christine Collette & Stephen Bird (eds), *Jews, Labour and the Left, 1918–48*, Ashgate, Aldershot, 2000, p. 71.

11   Emile Vandervelde, *Le Pays d'Israel. Un Marxiste en Palestine*, F Rieder, Paris, 1929, p. 9.

12   June Edmunds, *The Left and Israel: Party-Policy Change and Internal Democracy*, Macmillan, London, 2000, pp. 20–27.

13   British Labour Party Executive, 'A policy for Palestine', *Extract from the 'International Post-war Settlement' Report submitted to the 43rd Annual Conference*, 11–15 December 1944, London.

14   Paul Kelemen, *The British Left and Zionism: History of a divorce*, Manchester University Press, Manchester, 2012, pp. 111–28.

15   RHS Crossman and Michael Foot, *A Palestine Munich?*, Victor Gollancz, London, 1946.

16   Julius Braunthal, *In search of the Millennium*, Victor Gollancz, London, 1945, p. 305.

17   Yosef Gorny, *Converging Alternatives: The Bund and the Zionist Labor Movement, 1897-1985*, State University of New York Press, New York, 2006; Jack Jacobs, *Bundist Anti-Zionism in Interwar Poland*, Wallstein Verlag, Sonderdruck, 2005.

18   Philip Mendes, 'The Australian Left's support for the creation of the State of Israel, 1947–48', *Labour History*, 97, 2009, pp. 137–48.

19   Jonathan Judaken, *Jean-Paul Sartre and the Jewish Question*, University of Nebraska Press, Lincoln, 2006, p. 188.

20   Ronald Radosh and Allis Radosh, 'Righteous among the editors: When the Left loved Israel', *World Affairs*, 171, no.1, 2008, pp. 65–75.

21   Andrei Gromyko, *Address to United Nations General Assembly*, 1st Special Session, 77th Plenary Meeting, 14 May 1947, vol.1, pp. 127–35.

22   Laurent Rucker, *Moscow's Surprise: The Soviet-Israeli Alliance of 1947-1949*, Woodrow Wilson International Center for Scholars, Washington, 2005.

23   Benjamin Pinkus and Jonathan Frankel, *The Soviet Government and the Jews 1948-1967: A documented study*, Cambridge University Press, Cambridge, 1984.

24   Yoram Shapira, 'External and Internal Influences in Latin American-Israeli Relations', in Michael Curtis and Susan Aurelia Gitelson (eds), *Israel in the Third World*, Transaction Books, New Brunswick, 1976, pp. 152–53.

25   Colin Shindler, 'Old Lefts for New: Nye Bevan and Zion', *Jewish Quarterly*, vol. 32, no. 2, 1985, pp. 22–26.

26   Julius Braunthal, *The Significance of Israeli Socialism and the Arab-Israeli Dispute*, Lincolns-Prager, London, 1958, p. 17.

27   Braunthal, *The Significance of Israeli Socialism*, p. 27.

28   Edmunds, *The Left and Israel*, pp. 71–77.

29   Martin Luther King, 'Open letter to President Johnson', *New York Times*, 28 May 1967.

30   Judaken, *Jean-Paul Sartre and the Jewish Question*, pp. 195–96.

31   Seymour Martin Lipset, 'The Return of Anti-Semitism as a Political Force', in Irving Howe and Carl Gershman (eds), *Israel, The Arabs and the Middle East*, Bantam Books, New York, 1972, p. 417.

32   Philip Mendes, *The New Left, the Jews and the Vietnam War 1965-72*, Lazare Press, Melbourne, 1993, pp. 111–17.

33   Edmunds, *The Left and Israel*, pp. 92–93.

34   Stan Crooke, 'The Stalinist roots of left anti-Semitism', *Workers' Liberty*, no.10, May 1988, pp. 30–37.

35   Louis Shub, *The New Left and Israel*, Centre for the Study of Contemporary Jewish Life, Los Angeles, 1971, pp. 10–14.

36   Naomi Chazan, 'The quest for a two-state solution', *The Drum*, 17 June 2011, www.abc.net.au/news/2011-06-17/chazan---the-quest-for-a-two-state-solution/2760806.

37   Hillel Shenker, 'What's Wrong with BDS?', *Palestine-Israel Journal*, vol. 18, nos. 2 and 3, 2012, www.pij.org/details.php?id=1447.

38   See discussion in Philip Mendes, 'The Australian Greens and the Israeli-Palestinian conflict', in Dashiel Lawrence and Shahar Burla (eds), *Australia and Israel: A diasporic, cultural and political relationship*, Sussex Academic Press, Brighton, 2015.

39   Paul Berman, 'Something's changed: Bigotry in print. Crowds chant murder', in Ron Rosenbaum (ed.), *Those who forget the past: The question of Anti-Semitism*, Random House, New York, 2004.

40   David Hirsh, *Anti-Zionism and Antisemitism: Cosmopolitan Reflections*, Yale Initiative for the Interdisciplinary Study of Antisemitism Occasional Papers, New Haven, 2007.

41   Richard Ziegler, *The cults of Bosnia and Palestine*, Baico Publishing, Ottawa, 2012.

42 Pierre-Andre Taguieff, *Rising from the Muck: The New Anti-Semitism in Europe*, Ivan R Dee, Chicago, 2004.

2 The progressive case against Boycott, Divestment and Sanctions

1 'World Forum against Racism', NGO Forum Declaration, Durban, 3 September 2001, www.i-p-o.org/racism-ngo-decl.htm, accessed March 2014.

2 Stan Crooke, 'Boycott Apartheid Israel', in August Grabski (ed.), *Rebels Against Zion: Studies on the Jewish Left Anti-Zionism*, Jewish Institute of History, Warsaw, 2011, pp. 261–62; Harold Brackman, *Boycott Divestment Sanctions against Israel: An anti-Semitic, anti-peace poison pill*, Simon Wiesenthal Center, Los Angeles, 2013, p. 6.

3 Leslie Wagner, 'Watching the Pro-Israeli Academic Watchers', *Jewish Political Studies Review*, vol. 23, no. 12, 15 November 2010, www.jcpa.org/article/watching-the-pro-israeli-academic-watchers/, p. 2.

4 Lisa Taraki, 'Palestinian academics call for international academic boycott of Israel', *Birzeit University Right To Education Campaign Activism News*, 7 July 2004, www.right2edu.birzeit.edu/news/printer178.

5 Ramzyu Baroud, 'Palestine's global battle that must be won', in Rich Wiles (ed.), *Generation Palestine: Voices from the Boycott, Divestment and Sanctions Movement*, Pluto Press, London, 2013, pp. 13–14.

6 Palestinian Campaign for the Academic and Cultural Boycott of Israel, 'Guidelines for the International Academic Boycott of Israel', revised July 2014, www.pacbi.org/etemplate.php?id=1108, p.1.

7 Cary Nelson, 'The new assault on Israeli academia (and us)', *Fathom*, 22 September 2014.

8 Brackman, *Boycott Divestment Sanctions against Israel*, pp. 24–29; Omar Barghouti, 'Our South Africa Moment', in Moustafa Bayoumi (ed.), *Midnight on the Mavi Marmara: the attack on the Gaza Freedom Flotilla and How it Changed the Course of the Israel/Palestine Conflict*, Haymarket Books, Chicago, 2010, pp. 277–82; Scholars for Peace in the Middle East, *BDS Monitor*, 28 February 2014; Noura Erakat, 'Structural violence on trial: BDS and the movement to resist erasure', *Los Angeles Review of Books*, 16 March 2014, www.lareviewofbooks.org/essay/structural-violence-trial-bds-movement-resist-erasure, pp. 6–7.

9 Yoel Goldman, 'Universities quit US academic body over Israel boycott', *Times of Israel*, 19 December 2013, www.timesofisrael.com/schools-leave-academic-body-over-israel-boycott/.

10 Jeffrey Goldberg, 'Kerry's Israel boycott talk will backfire',

Bloomberg, 6 February 2014, www.bloombergview.com/
articles/2014-02-06/kerry-s-israel-boycott-talk-will-backfire.

11   Israeli GDP statistics can be viewed at www.imf.org/
external/pubs/ft/weo/2014/01/weodata/weorept.as-
px?sy=2014&ey=2014&scsm=1&ssd=1&sort=coun-
try&ds=.&br=1&c=436&s=NGDPD%2CNGDPDPC%2CPPPG-
DP%2CPPPPC&grp=0&a=&pr.x=75&pr.y=20 ; N Chazan (2011)
'The quest for a two-state solution'; David Rosenberg, 'Don't Buy
the Israel Boycott Hype', *Wall Street Journal Europe*, 27 February
2014, www.online.wsj.com/articles/SB10001424052702303426304
579402771597851680.

12   Author Unknown, 'A campaign that is gathering weight', *The
Economist*, 8 February 2014, www.economist.com/news/middle-
east-and-africa/21595948-israels-politicians-sound-rattled-
campaign-isolate-their-country/comments?page=2; Shlomo Maital,
'Dissecting BDS', *Jerusalem Report*, 24 (26),
7 April 2014, p. 36.

13   See www.pacbi.org/printnews.phd?id=869 for the July 2004
statement, and www.pacbi.org/printnews.php?id=66 for the July
2005 statement.

14   Hillel Shenker, 'What's Wrong with BDS?', *Palestine-Israel Journal*,
vol. 18, nos 2 and 3, 2012, www.pij.org/details.php?id=1447, p.
3; Peter Wertheim and Alex Ryvchin, *The Boycott, Divestment and
Sanctions (BDS) Campaign against Israel*, Executive Council of
Australian Jewry, Sydney, 2014, p. 4.

15   'Omar Barghouti: Co-founder of the Global BDS Movement &
PACBI interviewed', www.youtube.com/watch?v=qOBg2t6vscc ;
Roger Cohen, 'Zero Dark Zero', *New York Times*, 28 February 2013,
www.nytimes.com/2013/03/01/opinion/global/zero-dark-zero.html?_r=0,
accessed March 2014.

16   Alan Johnson, *The Apartheid Smear*, Britain/Israel Communications
& Research Centre, London, 2014,
www.static.bicom.org.uk/wp-content/uploads/2014/02/BICOM_
Apartheid-Smear_FINAL.pdf, p. 38.

17   Mustafa Barghouti, 'Freedom in our lifetime', in Audrea Lim (ed.),
The Case for Sanctions against Israel, Verso, London, 2012, pp. 3–4.

18   Alan Johnson, *The Apartheid Smear*, pp. 12–15.

19   Alan Johnson, *The Apartheid Smear*, pp. 11–12, 16–20; David Lloyd,
'What threatens Israel most? Democracy', *Los Angeles Review of
Books*, 16 March 2014, pp. 2–3.

20   Sonja Karkar, *Boycott Divestment Sanctions: A global campaign to end
Israeli Apartheid*, Australians for Palestine, Melbourne, 2010, p. 14;
Ilan Peleg and Dov Waxman, *Israel's Palestinians: The conflict within*,
Cambridge University Press, Cambridge, 2011, pp. 61–76; Daryl
Glaser, 'Zionism and Apartheid: a moral comparison', *Ethnic and
Racial Studies*, vol. 26, no. 3, 2003, p. 408.

21   Peleg and Waxman, *Israel's Palestinians*, pp. 183–88.
22   Mustafa Barghouti, 'Freedom in our lifetime', p. 4.
23   Noam Chomsky, 'On Israel-Palestine and BDS', *The Nation*, 2 July
      2014, www.thenation.com/article/180492/israel-palestine-and-bds.
24   GH Talhami, *Palestinian Refugees: Pawns to political actors*, Nova
      Science Publishers, New York, 2003, p. 15.
25   Robert Bowker, *Palestinian Refugees: Mythology, identity and the
      search for peace*, Lynne Rienner Publishers, Boulder, 2003, p. 98;
      Andrew Kent, 'Evaluating the Palestinians' Claimed Right of
      Return', *University of Pennsylvania Journal of International Law*,
      no. 34, 2012, pp. 172, 205.
26   Talhami, *Palestinian Refugees*, p. 15.
27   Talhami, *Palestinian Refugees*, pp. 155–56.
28   Benjamin Pogrund, 'Boycotts only harden Israeli opinion',
      Guardian, 24 August 2009.
29   Palestinian Campaign for the Academic and Cultural Boycott
      of Israel, 'Guidelines for the International Academic Boycott of
      Israel', revised July 2014, www.pacbi.org/etemplate.php?id=1108.
30   Crooke, 'Boycott Apartheid Israel', pp. 259–61.
31   Uri Avnery, 'Tutu's prayer', *Gush Shalom*, 31 August 2009, www.
      zope.gush-shalom.org/home/en/channels/avnery/1251547904/;
      Shlomo Gazit, 'Many instances of discrimination', *Bitterlemons*, no.
      8, 2012, www.bitterlemons-international.org/inside.php?id=1506,
      pp. 3–4.
32   Ali Mustafa, 'Boycotts work – an interview with Omar Barghouti',
      Electronic Intifada, 31 May 2009, www.electronicintifada.net/
      content/boycotts-work-interview-omar-barghouti/8263, p. 4.
33   Peleg and Waxman, *Israel's Palestinians*, p. 33; Johnson, *The
      Apartheid Smear*, pp. 6–9; Benjamin Pogrund, *Drawing Fire:
      Investigating The Accusations of Apartheid in Israel*, Rowman and
      Littlefield, Lanham, 2014, pp. 133–39.
34   Uri Avnery, 'Taking apartheid apart', *Gush Shalom*,
      26 October 2013, www.zope.gush-shalom.org/home/en/channels/
      avnery/1382707541/; Michael Lerner, 'Nelson Mandela: A Jewish
      perspective', *Tikkun Magazine online*,
      7 December 2013, www.tikkun.org/tikkundaily/2013/12/06/nelson-
      mandela-a-jewish-perspective/.
35   Hirsh, *Anti-Zionism and Antisemitism*, p. 97.
36   Johnson, *The Apartheid Smear*, pp. 8–9, 50–52.
37   Russell Berman, 'The goal of the boycott', *Los Angeles Review of
      Books*, 16 March 2014, pp. 1–11, www.lareviewofbooks.org/essay/
      goal-boycott ; MJ Rosenberg, 'The official goal of BDS is ending
      Israel, not just the '67 occupation', *Tikkun Daily*, 26 March 2014,
      www.tikkun.org/tikkundaily/2014/03/26/the-official-goal-of-bds-is-
      ending-israel-not-just-the-67-occupation/.
38   Omar Barghouti, 'Setting the record straight on BDS', *New*

Matilda, 2 May 2011.

39   Mustafa, 'Boycotts work', p. 5; Barghouti, *BDS*, pp. 178–79; M
      Barghouti (2012) 'Freedom in our lifetime', pp.10–11; Omar
      Barghouti, 'What comes next: A secular democratic state in historic
      Palestine – a promising land', *Mondoweiss*,
      21 October 2013, www.mondoweiss.net/2013/10/democratic-
      palestine-promising.

40   Moshe Machover, *Israelis and Palestinians*, Haymarket Books,
      Chicago, 2012, pp. 245, 288; Louis Shub, *The New Left and Israel*,
      Center for the Study of Contemporary Jewish Life, Los Angeles,
      1971, pp. 1, 3, 20.

41   Ali Abunimah, *One Country: A Bold Proposal to End the Israeli-
      Palestinian Impasse*, Metropolitan Books, New York, 2006,
      pp. 16, 105.

42   Ali Abunimah, *The Battle for Justice in Palestine*, Haymarket Books,
      Chicago, 2014, p. 232.

43   Noura Erakat, 'BDS in the USA, 2001-2010', in Audrea Lim (ed.),
      The Case for Sanctions against Israel, Verso, London, 2012, p. 87.

44   Bill V Mullen, 'Palestine, Boycott and Academic Freedom: A
      reassessment introduction', *AAUP Journal of Academic Freedom*,
      vol. 4, 2013, www.aaup.org/sites/default/files/files/JAF/2013%20
      JAF/Mullen.pdf, p. 1.

45   Anna Baltzer, *Witness in Palestine: Journal of a Jewish American
      Woman in the Occupied Territories*, Paradigm Publishers, Boulder,
      2006, p. 50.

46   Lloyd, 'What threatens Israel most? Democracy', pp. 4–5; Josh
      Ruebner, *Shattered Hopes: The Failure of Obama's Middle East Peace
      Process*, Verso, London, 2013, p. 288.

47   Peter Beinart, 'The real problem with the American Studies
      Association's Boycott of Israel', *Daily Beast*, 17 December 2013,
      www.thedailybeast.com/articles/2013/12/17/the-american-studies-
      association-is-really-boycotting-israel-s-existence.html.

48   Karkar, *Boycott Divestment Sanctions*, p. 27.

49   Danielle Peled, 'It's hard to be an anti-Zionist', *Jerusalem Report*, 16
      (3), 30 May 2005, pp. 25–26; David Aaronovitch, 'Why Israel will
      always be vilified', *Observer*, 24 April 2005, www.theguardian.com/
      education/2005/apr/24/highereducation.uk.

50   See, for example, comments by various BDS activists around the
      world including Samah Sabawi, 'A Palestinian woman's response
      to Israel's Naomi Chazan on BDS', *Mondoweiss*, 28 July 2011,
      www.mondoweiss.net/2011/07/samah-sabawi-a-palestinian-
      woman%E2%80%99s-response-to-naomi-chazan-on-bds ; Nadia
      Hijab, 'For human rights advocates, supporting BDS is a no-
      brainer', *Bitterlemons*, edition 22, 22 July 2011, www.bitterlemons-
      international.org/inside.php?id=1414.

51   Norman Finkelstein, 'Norman Finkelstein on BDS', *YouTube*,

15 February 2012, www.youtube.com/watch?v=iggdO7C70P8;
see also Norman Finkelstein, 'What comes next: If the goal is to
change U.S. policy, American Jewish opinion can't be ignored',
Mondoweiss, 22 October 2013, www.mondoweiss.net/2013/10/
american-opinion-ignored.

52 Yoel Goldman, 'Abbas: Don't boycott Israel', *Times of Israel*, 13
    December 2013, www.timesofisrael.com/abbas-we-do-not-support-
    the-boycott-of-israel/.

53 Alan Johnson, 'Bob Crow: a two states for two peoples
    trade unionist', *Left Foot Forward*, 11 March 2014,
    www.leftfootforward.org/2014/03; Eric Lee, 'Palestinians tell
    British union: Don't sever ties with the Histadrut', *Tulip Online*, 18
    April 2011, www.tuliponline.org/?p=3564.

54 Liz Ford, 'Boycotts self-defeating, Israel conference
    told', *Guardian*, 26 January 2006, www.theguardian.com/
    education/2006/jan/26/highereducation.uk1; Matthew Kalman,
    'Palestinians divided over boycott of Israeli universities', *New York
    Times*, 19 January 2014, www.nytimes.com/2014/01/20/world/
    middleeast/palestinians-divided-over-boycott-of-israeli-universities.
    html?_r=0.

55 Daoud Kuttab, 'The problems with boycotts', *Bitterlemons*, no.
    16, pp. 4–6, 2005, www.bitterlemons.org/previous/bl160505ed16.
    html pal2, p. 5.

56 Nelson, 'The problem with Judith Butler', p. 10.

57 David Toube, 'The real motive of the boycotters', *Jewish Chronicle*,
    21 February 2008, www.blog.peaceworks.net/2008/02/what-is-the-
    true-drive-and-motivation-behind-the-israel-boycott-movement/.

58 Barghouti, *BDS*, pp. 32, 80, 144–48.

59 Andy Beckett, 'It's water on stone – in the end the stone wears
    out', *Guardian*, 12 December 2002, www.theguardian.com/
    education/2002/dec/12/highereducation.uk; Jonathan Freedland,
    'Firing on our friends', *Guardian*, 8 July 2002, www.theguardian.
    com/education/2002/jul/10/highereducation.uk1; Edward
    Alexander, *The State of the Jews: A Critical Appraisal*, Transaction
    Publishers, New Brunswick, 2012, pp. 142–43.

60 David Landy, *Jewish identity and Palestinian rights: Diaspora Jewish
    opposition to Israel*, Zed Books, London, 2011, pp. 16, 87, 174, 224.

61 Donna Nevel, 'Boycott, Divestment and Sanctions (BDS) and
    the American Jewish Community', *Tikkun Daily*, 7 March 2014,
    www.tikkun.org/tikkundaily/2014/03/07/boycott-divestment-and-
    sanctions-bds-and-the-american-jewish-community/.

62 Erakat, 'Structural violence on trial', p. 7.

63 Curthoys, 'An argument for a moratorium', p. 26.

64 Sabawi, 'A Palestinian woman's response to Naomi Chazan on
    BDS'. For a similar attack on Chazan by another Australian BDS
    supporter, see Mira Adler-Gillies, 'BDS a last resort counter to

Israeli exceptionalism', *The Drum*, 21 June 2011, www.abc.net.au/news/2011-04-05/adlergillesisrael/55352.

65   Karkar, *Boycott Divestment Sanctions*, p. 26.

66   Saul Friedlander, *Nazi Germany and the Jews: Volume 1: The Years of Persecution: 1933-1939*, Harper Collins, New York, 1997, pp. 49–60; Julius, *Trials of the Diaspora*, pp. 478–83.

67   Martin A Weiss, *Arab League Boycott of Israel*, Congressional Research Service, Washington, 2013, www.fpc.state.gov/documents/organization/219630.pdf , p. 4.

68   Abigail Bakan and Yameen Abu-Laban, 'Palestinian resistance and international solidarity: the BDS campaign', *Race & Class*, vol. 51, no. 1, 2009, pp. 33–38.

69   Dave Rich, 'Campus War 1977: The year that Jewish societies were banned', in Alvin H Rosenfeld (ed.), *Resurgent Antisemitism*, Indiana University Press, Bloomington, 2013, pp. 255–76.

70   Christopher Hitchens, 'Anti-Semitism: The Socialism of Fools', *New Statesman*, 20 June 1980, p. 928; August Bebel, 'Assassinations and socialism', from a speech delivered by August Bebel, delivered at Berlin, November 2, 1898 (translated by Boris Reinstein), New York Labor News Company, New York, c. 1898, www.archive.org/details/assassinationsso00bebeuoft .

71   Palestinian BDS National Committee, 'BNC condemns repression of BDS activism in Australia', 17 August 2011, www.bdsmovement.net/2011/bnc-condemns-repression-of-bds-activism-in-australia-7866.

72   Randa Abdel-Fattah, 'Who's afraid of BDS? Israel's assault on academic freedom', *ABC Religion and Ethics*, 31 October 2013, www.abc.net.au/religion/articles/2013/10/31/3880687.htm ; Kim Bullimore, 'BDS and the struggle for a free Palestine', in Antony Loewenstein and Jeff Sparrow (eds), *Left Turn: Political essays for the new left*, Melbourne University Press, Melbourne, 2012, p. 204; Antony Loewenstein, 'To support the boycott, divestment and sanctions movement is not antisemitic', *Guardian*, 8 November 2013, www.theguardian.com/commentisfree/2013/nov/07/to-support-the-boycott-divestment-and-sanctions-movement-is-not-anti-semitic; Stuart Rees, 'Defending the right to dissent', *New Matilda*, 12 August 2013, www.newmatilda.com/2013/08/12/defending-right-dissent; Peter Slezak, 'Anti-Semitism and BDS; Beyond misrepresentations', *ABC Religion and Ethics*, 15 November 2013, www.abc.net.au/religion/articles/2013/11/15/3891979.htm.

73   Antony Loewenstein, 'Why boycotting Israel matters', *The Drum*, 18 December 2012, www.abc.net.au/news/2012-12-18/lowenstein-bds/4433598.

74   Landy, *Jewish Identity and Palestinian Rights*, pp.108, 165.

75   Steven Salaita, 'Ten things we've learned about opposition to

academic boycott', *Electronic Intafada*, 14 January 2014, www.electronicintifada.net/blogs/steven-salaita/ten-things-weve-learned-about-opposition-academic-boycott.

76   Hirsh, *Anti-Zionism and Antisemitism*, pp.11, 53–57.

77   Paul Kelemen, *The British Left and Zionism: History of a divorce*, Manchester University Press, Manchester, 2012, p. 187.

78   Ben Gidley, 'The politics of defining racism: The case of Anti-Semitism in the University and College Union', *Dissent*, 26 May 2011, www.dissentmagazine.org/blog/the-politics-of-defining-racism-the-case-of-anti-semitism-in-the-university-and-college-union, pp. 2–3.

79   Gidley, 'The politics of defining racism', pp. 5–7.

80   Verashni Pillay, 'Shoot the Jew song slammed', *Mail and Guardian*, www.mg.co.za/article/2013-09-02-shoot-the-jew-song-slammed/.

81   Jewish Telegraphic Agency, 'Dutch pro-Palestine group defends "Jews control Internet" article', *Haaretz*, 10 February 2014, www.haaretz.com/jewish-world/jewish-world-news/1.573457.

82   Ean Higgins and Christian Kerr, 'Jihad Sheila link to anti-Jewish posts', *The Australian*, 3 May 2013, www.theaustralian.com.au/national-affairs/foreign-affairs/jihad-sheila-link-to-anti-jewish-posts/story-fn59nm2j-1226634265874; Christian Kerr, 'PM denounces activists as anti-Israel protest turns anti-Semitic', *The Australian*, 30 April 2013, www.theaustralian.com.au/higher-education/julia-gillard-denounces-activists-as-anti-israel-protest-turns-anti-semitic/story-e6frgcjx-1226631889398; Daniel Meyerowitz-Katz, 'Sue me Jew: Horrific hate-speech by Australian students on anti-Israel Facebook page', 29 April 2013, www.aijac.org.au/news/article/sue-me-jew-horrific-hate-speech-by-australian-st; Peter Wertheim and Julie Nathan, 'The ugly face of student activism', *The Australian*, 30 April 2013, www.theaustralian.com.au/national-affairs/opinion/the-ugly-face-of-student-activism/story-e6frgd0x-1226631853245.

83   Antony Loewenstein, 'Australian unions, Paul Howes, BDS and loving Israel', *Crikey.com*, 11 November 2010, www.antony.wpmu.wud-web.com/2010/11/11/australian-unions-paul-howes-bds-and-loving-israel/.

84   Paul Howes, 'Radicalism may force Greens to change tunes', *Sunday Telegraph*, 3 April 2011, www.dailytelegraph.com.au/radicalism-may-force-greens-to-change/story-fn6b3v4f-1226032636625?nk=1b47935c0e323e508852f6800b5151f0.

85   Antony Loewenstein, 'Marrickville madness over BDS but Palestinian rights aren't forgotten', www.antonyloewenstein.com/2011/04/20/marrickville-madness-over-bds-but-palestine-rights-arent-forgotten/.

86   Stuart Rees, 'The Israel lobby's goal is silence', *New Matilda*, 15

April 2014, https://newmatilda.com/2014/04/15/israel-lobbys-goal-silence.

87   Vacy Vlazna, 'Wherefore by their friends ye shall know them: Zionists vs UNSW BDS', *Palestine Chronicle*, 7 May 2013, www.palestinechronicle.com/wherefore-by-their-friends-ye-shall-know-them-zionists-vs-unsw-bds .

88   Jake Lynch, 'Toeing the Lobby Line', *New Matilda*, 8 February 2011, www.newmatilda.com/2011/02/08/toeing-lobby-line; Jake Lynch, 'Can the centre hold? Prospects for mobilizing media activism around public service broadcasting using peace journalism', in Ibrahim Seaga Shaw, Jake Lynch and Robert A Hackett (eds), *Expanding peace journalism: comparative and critical approaches*, Sydney University Press, Sydney, 2010, p. 290.

89   Mona Baker and Lawrence Davidson, 'In Defense of the Boycott of Israeli Academic Institutions', *Counterpunch*, 17 September 2003, www.counterpunch.org/2003/09/17/in-defense-of-the-boycott-of-israeli-academic-institutions/.

90   Stephen H Norwood, *Antisemitism and the American Far Left*, Cambridge University Press, New York, 2013, p. 219; Robert Wistrich, 'A deadly mutation: Antisemitism and Anti-Zionism in Great Britain', in Eunice Pollack (ed.), *Antisemitism on the Campus: Past & Present*, Academic Studies Press, Boston, 2011, p. 63.

91   Daniel Meyerowitz-Katz, 'Incitement watch: BDS harasses synagogue-goers in the US while Arabic media see Jewish plots everywhere', 13 June 2013, www.aijac.org.au/news/article/incitement-watch-bds-group-harasses-synagogue-go.

92   Peter Kohn, 'BDS supporters cancel synagogue demonstration', *Australian Jewish News*, 17 February 2012, www.jewishnews.net.au/bds-supporters-cancel-synagogue-demonstration/24895.

93   Karkar, *Boycott Divestment Sanctions*, pp. 10, 25.

94   Omar Barghouti, 'The pianist of Palestine', *Counterpunch*, 29 November 2004, www.counterpunch.org/2004/11/29/quot-the-pianist-quot-of-palestine/.

95   Frank Barat, 'An Interview with Roger Waters', *Counterpunch*, Weekend Edition: 6–8 December 2013, www.counterpunch.org/2013/12/06/an-interview-with-pink-floyds-roger-waters/.

96   Shalom Lappin, 'Why I resigned from the AUT', 28 April 2005, www.normblog.typepad.com/normblog/2005/04/why_i_resigned_.html.

97   Adam Kredo, 'Palestinian activists violently threaten pro-Israel students', *The Washington Free Beacon*, 21 March 2014, www.freebeacon.com/national-security/palestinian-activists-violently-threaten-pro-israel-students/.

98   Alan Johnson, 'BDS bullies at Galway University', *Times of Israel*, 10 March 2014, www.blogs.timesofisrael.com/bds-bullies-at-

galway-university/.

99 Israel Central Bureau of Statistics, *Selected data on the occasion of Jerusalem Day*, 2014, www1.cbs.gov.il/www/ hodaot2013n/11_13_119e.pdf.

100 Jonah Shepp, 'Why we Jews get so worked up over BDS', 24 December 2013, www.blog.partners4israel.org/2013/12/why-we-jews-get-so-worked-up-over-bds_24.html.

101 David Graham and Jonathan Boyd, *Committed, concerned and conciliatory: the attitudes of Jews in Britain towards Israel*, Institute for Jewish Policy Research, London, 2010; Andrew Markus, Nicky Jacobs and Tanya Aronov, *2008-9 Jewish Population Survey*, Monash University Australian Centre for Jewish Civilisation, Melbourne, 2008, pp. 15–17; Leonard Saxe, Theodore Sasson, Shahar Hecht and Benjamin Phillips, *Still Connected: American Jewish Attitudes about Israel*, Brandeis University, 2010.

102 Markus, Jacobs and Aronov, pp. 15–17.

103 David Hirsh, 'Civility in contemporary debates about anti-Semitism,' *Jewish Quarterly*, vol. 61, no. 1, Spring 2014, pp. 38–39.

104 Barghouti, *BDS*, p. 149.

105 Barghouti, *BDS*, p. 60.

106 Baker and Davidson, 'In defense of the boycott of Israeli academic institutions', p. 2.

107 Landy, *Jewish Identity and Palestinian Rights*, p. 155.

108 Academics for Palestine, *Academia against apartheid: The case for an academic boycott of Israel*, 19 February 2014, www.academicsforpalestine.wordpress.com, p. 15.

109 Ilan Pappe, 'Colonialism, the peace process and the academic boycott', in Rich Wiles (ed.), *Generation Palestine*, Pluto Press, London, 2013, p. 137.

110 Bakan and Abu-Laban, 'Palestinian resistance', pp. 43–46.

111 Ned Curthoys, John Docker and Antony Loewenstein, 'Palestine's Ghandi – Omar Barghouti, BDS and int'l [sic] law', *Overland Blog*, 31 May 2011, www.overland.org.au/2011/05/palestine%E2%80%99s-gandhi-omar-barghouti-bds-and-int%E2%80%99l-humanitarian-law/, p. 4.

112 Paul Duffill and Gabriella Scoff, 'Growing Jewish support for boycott and the changing landscape of the BDS debate', *Mondoweiss*, 17 June 2014, www.mondoweiss.net/2014/06/boycott-changing-landscape.html.

113 Philip Mendes, *Jews and the Left: The rise and fall of a political alliance*, Palgrave Macmillan, London, 2014, Chapters 2 and 8.

114 Hirsh, *Anti-Zionism and Antisemitism*, pp. 109–110, 120; Anthony Julius, *Trials of the Diaspora*, Oxford University Press, Oxford, 2010, pp. 557–59; Emanuele Ottolenghi, 'Present-day Antisemitism and the centrality of the Jewish alibi', in Alvin H

Rosenfeld (ed.), *Resurgent Antisemitism*, Indiana University Press, Bloomington, 2013, p. 440.

115 Carolyn Karcher, 'Why I voted for an academic boycott of Israel', *Los Angeles Times*, 27 December 2013, www.articles. latimes.com/2013/dec/27/news/la-ol-israel-academic-boycott-blowback-20131227.

116 Hirsh, *Anti-Zionism and Antisemitism*, p. 13. For a similar argument from an Australian left-wing academic, see Andrew Jakubowicz, 'Civility and terror in academic life: The Israeli academic boycotts', *Borderlands*, vol. 2, no. 3, pp. 1–10, 2003, www.borderlands.net.au/vol2no3_2003/jakubowicz.htm, p. 4.

117 Mendes, *Jews and the Left*, chapter 8; Anthony Julius, *Trials of the Diaspora*, Oxford University Press, Oxford, 2010, pp. 555–57; Dave Rich, 'Campus War 1977: The year that Jewish societies were banned', in Alvin H Rosenfeld (ed.), *Resurgent Antisemitism*, Indiana University Press, Bloomington, 2013, p. 268.

118 Barghouti, *BDS*, p.171; Omar Barghouti, 'The cultural boycott: Israel vs South Africa', in Audrea Lim (ed.), *The Case for Sanctions against Israel*, Verso, London, 2011, p. 31; Barghouti cited in Mustafa, 'Boycotts work', p. 2; Ghada Karmi, 'The weapon of the weak', *Bitterlemons*, no. 26, pp. 3–4, www.bitterlemons-international.org/inside.php?id=765, p. 3.

119 Palestinian BDS National Committee, 'BNC condemns repression of BDS activism in Australia', 17 August 2011, www.bdsmovement.net/2011/bnc-condemns-repression-of-bds-activism-in-australia-7866.

120 Palestinian BDS National Committee, 'BDS movement position on boycott of individuals', 21 February 2013, www.bdsmovement.net/2013/bds-movement-position-on-boycott-of-individuals-10679.

121 Bullimore, 'BDS and the struggle for a free Palestine', p. 199.

122 Robert Fine, 'Address to Leeds University BDS debate', *Engage Online*, 21 March 2014, www.engageonline.wordpress.com/2014/03/21/robert-fine-debates-the-boycotters-in-leeds/.

123 Ari Y Kelman, 'Engage, Don't Boycott: An open letter to the American Studies Association', *The Nation*, 13 December 2013, www.thenation.com/article/177590/engage-dont-boycott-open-letter-american-studies-association; Cary Nelson, 'The problem with Judith Butler: The political philosophy of the movement to boycott Israel', *Los Angeles Review of Books*, 16 March 2014, pp. 1–21, www.lareviewofbooks.org/essay/problem-judith-butler-political-philosophy-movement-boycott-israel, p. 2.

124 Palestinian Campaign for the Academic and Cultural Boycott of Israel, 'Guidelines for the International Academic Boycott of Israel', revised July 2014, www.pacbi.org/etemplate.php?id=1108.

125 PACBI cited in Karkar, *Boycott Divestment Sanctions*, p. 29.

126 Alexander, *The State of the Jews*, p. 140; Engage, 'Why boycott Israeli Universities? A response to Bricup', Engage Online, May 2007, www.engageonline.org.uk/ressources/bricup/why_boycott_a_response_to_bricup.pdf, p. 10.

127 Polly Curtis, 'Suspension not enough for Oxford don, say students', *Guardian*, 28 October 2003, www.theguardian.com/education/2003/oct/28/internationaleducationnews.highereducation; Julie Henry, 'Outrage as Oxford bans student for being Israeli', *Daily Telegraph*, 29 June 2003, www.telegraph.co.uk/news/worldnews/africaandindianocean/liberia/1434388/Outrage-as-Oxford-bans-student-for-being-Israeli.html.

128 David Hirsh, 'The American Studies Association boycott resolution, academic freedom and the myth of the institutional boycott', *Engage Online*, 7 January 2014, www.engageonline.wordpress.com/2014/01/07/the-american-studie..., p. 4.

129 Cahal Milmo, 'Jewish academic Moty Crista sues Unison for racial discrimination', *Independent*, 12 September 2013, www.independent.co.uk/news/uk/home-news/jewish-academic-moty-cristal-sues-unisonfor-racial-discrimination-8810113.html.

130 Adam Withnall, 'George Galloway declares Bradford an Israel-free zone and warns away Israeli tourists', *Independent*, 7 August 2014, www.independent.co.uk/news/uk/politics/george-galloway-declares-bradford-an-israelfree-zone-9653894.html.

131 Marjorie Heins, 'Rethinking Academic Boycotts', *AAUP Journal of Academic Freedom*, vol. 4, 2013, pp. 1–12, www.aaup.org/sites/default/files/JAF/2013%20JAF/Heins.pdf, p. 7.

132 Judith Butler, 'Israel/Palestine and the paradoxes of academic freedom', *Radical Philosophy*, vol. 135, January/February 2006, p. 9.

133 Hirsh, *Anti-Zionism and Antisemitism*, pp. 111–12.

134 Steve Cohen, 'I would hate myself in the morning', *Engage Online*, 29 May 2006, www.engageonline.org.uk/blog/article.php?id=444.

135 Baruch Kimmerling, 'The meaning of academic boycott', *Borderlands*, vol. 2, no. 3, 2003, pp. 1–10, www.borderlands.net.au/vol2no3_2003/kimmerling_meaning.htm, p. 2.

136 David Myers, 'Why I oppose a boycott, mostly', *Los Angeles Review of Books*, 16 March 2014, pp. 1–8, www.lareviewofbooks.org/essay/oppose-boycott-mostly.

137 Michael Yudkin, 'Is an academic boycott of Israel justified?', *Engage Journal*, April 2007, www.engageonline.org.uk/journal/index.php?journal_id=15&article_id=61, pp. 7–8.

138 Baruch Kimmerling, 'The meaning of academic boycott', *Z Net*, 26 April 2005.

139 Dean Sherr, 'Boycott boon to Israel's Right', *The Australian*, 5 November 2013, www.theaustralian.com.au/national-

affairs/opinion/boycott-boon-to-israels-right/story-
e6frgd0x-1226753047229.

140 Chazan, 'The quest for a two-state solution'. See also Naomi
Chazan, 'BDS, the boycott law and Israel's democracy',
Bitterlemons, 21 July 2011, Edition 22, www.bitterlemons-
international.org/inside.php?id=1415, p. 2.

141 Eric Alterman, 'Despicable Me', *The Nation*, 23 October 2013,
www.thenation.com/blog/176770/despicable-me.

142 David Newman, 'The ultimatum set by the University of
Johannesburg for Ben Gurion University', *Jerusalem Post*, 4 October
2010, www.jpost.com/Opinion/Columnists/Borderline-views-The-
wrong-litmus-test.

3 Case study: BDS in Australia

1   WD Rubinstein, *The Jews in Australia: A Thematic History, Volume
Two*, William Heinemann Australia, Melbourne, 1991, p. 69.

2   John Docker, 'Thirteen untimely meditations', *Arena Magazine*,
no. 55, 2001, p. 11. See also Philip Mendes, (2003) 'Denying
the Jewish Experience of Oppression: the Jewish anti-Zionism of
John Docker', *Australian Journal of Jewish Studies*, 17, pp. 112–130;
Ghassan Hage, *Against Paranoid Nationalism*, Pluto Press, Sydney,
2002, pp. 123, 128, 129 & 136.

3   John Docker and Ghassan Hage, 'Boycott just the way to rap
Israel', *The Australian*, 22 May 2002.

4   Andrew Jakubowicz, 'Anatomy of a boycott', *Sydney
Morning Herald*, 8 February 2003, www.smh.com.au/
articles/2003/02/07/1044579925054.html.

5   Alan Borowski et al, 'Boycott of Israel would penalise those most
needed', *The Australian*, 29 May 2002.

6   Alon Lee, 'Academics fight back on Israel boycott bid', *Australian
Jewish News*, 31 May 2002.

7   Lee, 'Academics fight back on Israel boycott bid'.

8   Graeme McCulloch, 'Editorial note', *NTEU Advocate*, no. 6,
November 2012, www.issuu.com/nteu/docs/advocate_19_03, p.
6; Ean Higgins, 'Israel sanctions backers miffed', *The Australian*,
11 June 2014, www.theaustralian.com.au/higher-education/israel-
sanctions-backers-miffed/story-e6frgcjx-1226949822263.

9   Tom Hyland, 'Row over Israeli chocolate leaves a bitter taste',
The Age, 18 September 2011, www.theage.com.au/victoria/row-
over-israeli-chocolate-leaves-a-bitter-taste-20110917-1kf20.html;
Executive Council of Australian Jewry, 'ECAJ urges restraint in
rhetoric', 14 September 2011, www.ecaj.org.au/2011/ecaj-urges-
restraint-in-rhetoric/.

10   Kim Bullimore, 'BDS and the struggle for a free Palestine', in
Antony Loewenstein and Jeff Sparrow (eds), *Left Turn: Political
essays for the new left*, Melbourne University Press, Melbourne,

2012, p. 203; Karkar, *Boycott Divestment Sanctions*, p. 49.

11   Cameron Stewart, 'Anti-Israel bullies' hard centre bites in
      chocolate shop campaign', *The Australian*, 20 August 2011,
      www.theaustralian.com.au/national-affairs/opinion/anti-israel-
      bullies-hard-centre-bites-in-chocolate-shop-campaign/story-
      e6frgd0x-1226118406097; Christian Kerr, 'Protests lack link to
      Israel: BDS fan', *The Australian*, 2 May 2013, www.theaustralian.
      com.au/national-affairs/foreign-affairs/protests-lack-link-to-israel-
      bds-fan/story-fn59nm2j-1226633490418.

12   Timna Jacks, 'Israel supporters take to Melbourne streets',
      Australian Jewish News, 9 September 2011, www.jewishnews.net.au/
      israel-supporters-take-to-melbourne-streets/22761.

13   Doug Kirsner, Ari Suss and Geoffrey Winn, 'Hot chocolate a cure
      for those who ignore history', *The Punch*, 23 August 2011.

14   Michael Danby, 'Anti-Israel protests don't deserve support', *Herald
      Sun*, 27 July 2012, www.blogs.news.com.au/heraldsun/law/index.
      php/heraldsun/comments/anti_israel_protests_dont_deserve_
      support/.

15   Rick Morton, 'Diplomacy better than Israel boycott: Rudd', *The
      Australian*, 17 January 2013, www.theaustralian.com.au/national-
      affairs/targeting-jewish-businesses-just-wrong/story-fn59niix-
      1226555410832&memtype=anonymous.

16   Christian Kerr, 'PM denounces activists as anti-Israel protest turns
      anti-Semitic', *The Australian*, 30 April 2013, www.theaustralian.
      com.au/higher-education/julia-gillard-denounces-activists-as-anti-
      israel-protest-turns-anti-semitic/story-e6frgcjx-1226631889398.

17   Leo Shanahan, 'Anti-Jew protest condemned', *The Australian*, 28
      July.

18   Stewart, 'Anti-Israel bullies'.

19   AJDS Executive, 'AJDS statement update regarding BDS protests',
      18 September 2011, www.ajds.org.au/node/424.

20   Daniel Meyerowitz-Katz, 'Sue me Jew: Horrific hate-speech by
      Australian students on anti-Israel Facebook page', 29 April 2013,
      www.aijac.org.au/news/article/sue-me-jew-horrific-hate-speech-by-
      australian-st; Peter Wertheim and Julie Nathan, 'The ugly face of
      student activism', *The Australian*, 30 April 2013, www.theaustralian.
      com.au/national-affairs/opinion/the-ugly-face-of-student-activism/
      story-e6frgd0x-1226631853245.

21   AJDS Executive, AJDS statement update regarding BDS protests.

22   Pia Akerman and John Ferguson, 'Baillieu seeks to toughen protest
      laws', *The Australian*, 25 July 2012, www.theaustralian.com.au/
      national-affairs/state-politics/baillieu-seeks-to-toughen-protest-
      laws/story-e6frgczx-1226434242358.

23   Louise Perry and Megan Saunders, 'Vote on Ashrawi award not
      split', *The Australian*, 24 October 2003.

24   Stuart Rees, 'A craven approach to peace and justice',

Sydney Morning Herald, 22 October 2013, www.smh.com.au/
articles/2003/10/21/1066631429075.html?from=storyrhs.

25   Alan Ramsey, 'Here's Lucy, caving in, taking flight', *Sydney
     Morning Herald*, 25 October 2003, www.smh.com.au/
     articles/2003/10/24/1066974313719.html.

26   Jake Lynch, *Debates in Peace Journalism*, Sydney University Press,
     Sydney, 2008, pp. 184–88.

27   Philip Mendes, 'Advocating peace or promoting conflict and
     discrimination? The strange case of the Centre for Peace and
     Conflict Studies', *Galus Australis*, 23 March 2011,
     www.galusaustralis.com/2011/03/4254/advocating-peace-or-
     promoting-conflict-and-discrimination-the-strange-case-of-the-
     centre-for-peace-and-conflict-studies.

28   Jake Lynch, 'Toeing the Lobby Line', *New Matilda*,
     8 February 2011, www.newmatilda.com/2011/02/08/toeing-lobby-
     line.

29   Peter Hartcher, 'What am I, chopped liver? How Rudd dived into
     Schmooze mode', *Sydney Morning Herald*, 22 June 2010, www.smh.
     com.au/federal-politics/political-opinion/what-am-i-chopped-liver-
     how-rudd-dived-into-schmooze-mode-20100621-ys5g.html.

30   For a list of Jewish visitors, see Paul Duffill, 'Establishing the
     facts about the boycott of Israeli academic institutions', *The
     Conversation*, 15 January 2013, www.theconversation.com/
     establishing-the-facts-about-the-boycott-of-israeli-academic-
     institutions-11565.

31   Stuart Rees, 'Truth, justice, peace: The moral and legal foundations
     of the BDS movement', *ABC Religion and Ethics*, 20 November
     2013, www.abc.net.au/religion/articles/2013/11/20/3895305.htm.

32   Centre for Peace and Conflict Studies, 2009 *Annual Report*,
     University of Sydney, Sydney, www.sydney.edu.au/arts/peace_
     conflict/about/2009%20Annual%20Report.pdf, p.19.

33   Christian Kerr, 'Uni peace centre rebuffs Israeli civics teacher', *The
     Australian*, 6 December 2012, www.theaustralian.com.au/higher-
     education/sydney-university-peace-centre-rebuffs-israeli-civics-
     teacher/story-e6frgcjx-1226530838896; Christian Kerr, 'Centre
     chief rebuked over snub to Israeli', *The Australian*, 8 December.

34   Christian Kerr, 'Sydney University rejects call for Israel boycott',
     The Australian, 10 May 2013, www.theaustralian.com.au/
     higher-education/boycotts-campaign-formally-rejected/story-
     e6frgcjx-1226638941057.

35   Yonah Jeremy Bob, 'Australian Professor: Law group sued me
     because BDS works', *The Jerusalem Post*, 27 August 2013, www.
     jpost.com/Diplomacy-and-Politics/Australian-professor-Law-
     group-sued-me-because-BDS-works-324463; Nick Dyrenfurth,
     'Boycotting Israel another impediment to peace', *The Saturday
     Paper*, 19 April 2014, www.thesaturdaypaper.com.au/opinion/

topic/2014/04/19/boycotting-israel-another-impediment-peace/1397829600.U2DvwfmSx8k; Christian Kerr, 'Anti-Israel lobby defiant on uni rally', *The Australian*, 28 August 2013, www.theaustralian.com.au/news/nation/anti-israel-lobby-defiant-on-uni-rally/story-e6frg6nf-1226705314930; Dan Goldberg, 'Australian court case fires up BDS campaign against Israel', *Haaretz*, 30 April 2013, www.haaretz.com/jewish-world/jewish-world-news/.premium-1.588059; Ean Higgins, 'BDS vindicated by Israeli activists loss', *The Australian*, 16 July 2014, www.theaustralian.com.au/higher-education/bds-vindicated-by-israeli-activists-loss/story-e6frgcjx-1226990122883.

36   Philip Mendes, 'The Australian Greens: Taking Sides on the Israeli/Palestinian Conflict', *B'nai B'rith Anti-Defamation Commission Special Report*, No. 22, September 2004.

37   Imre Salusinzky, 'Israeli boycott debate splits state's Greens', *The Australian*, 16 September 2011, www.theaustralian.com.au/national-affairs/state-politics/israeli-boycott-debate-splits-states-greens/story-e6frgczx-1226138271245; Gareth Narunsky, 'New Greens leader: BDS is behind us', *Australian Jewish News*, 20 April 2012, www.jewishnews.net.au/new-greens-leader-bds-is-behind-us/25824; Sean Nicholls and Jo Tovey, 'Anti-Israel boycott opens fresh split in Greens', *Sydney Morning Herald*, 9 September 2011, www.smh.com.au/nsw/antiisrael-boycott-opens-fresh-split-in-greens-20110908-1jzy7.html; Peter Wertheim, *Executive Council of Australian Jewry Annual Report* (2013), ECAJ, Sydney, 2013, pp. 88–91; Sally Neighbour, 'Divided we fall', *The Monthly*, February 2012, pp. 21–28.

38   Lee Rhiannon, 'Adjournment speech: Ceasing Australian military co-operation with Israel', *Hansard Senate*, 4 December 2013, www.lee-rhiannon.greensmps.org.au.

39   Paul Maley, 'Council boycott of Israel self-indulgent', *The Australian*, 13 January 2011, www.theaustralian.com.au/news/nation/council-boycott-of-israel-self-indulgent/story-e6frg6nf-1225986604144.

40   Simon Holt, 'Marrickville's boycott of Israel blasted by PM Julia Gillard', *Inner West Courier*, 11 May 2011.

41   Maley, 'Council boycott of Israel'.

42   Australian Senate, 'Israel: Boycotts', *Hansard Senate*, 24 March 2011, www.aph.gov.au/hansard/senate/dailys/ds230311.pdf.

43   Jack Passaris, 'Letter to Marrickville Council Mayor Fiona Byrne' in Peter Wertheim, *BDS suffers a defeat in Australia*, 2011, p. 28.

44   Matthew Franklin and Amos Aikman, 'Anti-Israel stance focus of Greens review', *The Australian*, 28 March 2011, www.theaustralian.com.au/national-affairs/anti-israeli-stance-focus-of-greens-review/story-fn59niix-1226029042280?nk=1b47935c0e323e508852f6800b5151f0; Imre Salusinszky and Leo Shanahan, 'Boycott

call cost Greens state seat', *The Australian*, 15 April 2011, www.
theaustralian.com.au/national-affairs/boycott-call-cost-greens-state-
seat-in-marrickville/story-fn59niix-1226039401886.

45   Amos Aikman and Leo Shanahan, 'Greens forced to back
down on boycott', *The Australian*, 20 April 2011, www.theaus-
tralian.com.au/national-affairs/marrickville-council-drops-is-
rael-boycott/story-fn59niix-1226041840517?nk=a8b7795dcd-
8492c2a06b08020ed9d831.

46   Marrickville Council, *Minutes of Council Meeting*, 19 April 2011,
www.marrickville.nsw.gov.au/en/council/elected-council/business-
paper-archives/council-meetings/.

47   Jo Tovey, 'Greens abandon official support for Israel boycott',
Sydney Morning Herald, 5 December 2011, www.smh.com.au/
nsw/greens-abandon-official-support-for-israel-boycott-20111205-
1odzh.html ixzz1h0qJP43y.

48   David Speers, 'The Nation', *Sky News*, 14 April 2011,
www.youtube.com/watch?v=4CbHAhGl2L0.

49   Fiona Byrne, 'Taking local action on international issues', *The Drum
Unleashed*, 13 January 2011, www.abc.net.au/unleashed/42988.
html.

50   Peter Wertheim, *BDS suffers a defeat in Australia: The Marrickville
Council Controversy*, Executive Council of Australian Jewry, Sydney,
2011, pp. 13–14, 26–27, 36–37, 65–66; Gael Kennedy and Janet
Kossy, 'Councils can help Mid-East peace', *National Times*, 19 April
2011, www.smh.com.au/it-pro/councils-can-help-mideast-peace-
20110418-1dlj9.html.

51   Peter Slezak, 'Anti-Semitism and BDS; Beyond
misrepresentations', *ABC Religion and Ethics*, 15 November 2013,
www.abc.net.au/religion/articles/2013/11/15/3891979.htm.

52   Philip Mendes, 'Australian Jewish Dissent on Israel: A History
of the Australian Jewish Democratic Society (Part 1)', *Australian
Jewish Historical Society Journal*, November 1999, pp. 117–38.

53   Sol Salbe, 'AJDS endorses nuanced version of BDS', *AJDS
Newsletter*, vol. 11, no. 7, 2010, p. 3, www.ajds.org.au/wp-content/
uploads/Newsletter%20August%202010.pdf; Sol Salbe, 'The
AJDS responds to the Jewish Community Council of Victoria',
September/October 2010, www.docstoc.com/docs/83434914/
Newsletter-September-October-2010 , p. 3; Landy, *Jewish Identity
and Palestinian Rights*, pp. 101, 162.

54   Harold Zwier, 'Why I resigned from the AJDS Executive', *AJDS
Newsletter*, vol. 11, no. 8, 2010, p. 4, http://www.docstoc.com/
docs/83434914/Newsletter-September-October-2010.

55   Larry Stillman, 'AJDS criticizes disruptive BDS protests', 8
September 2011, email newsletter delivered via info@ajds.org.au.

56   Australian Jewish Democratic Society, 'Statement on the JCCV's
threatened disaffiliation', 6 May 2013, www.ajds.org.au/ajds-

statement-on-the-jccvs-threatened-disaffiliation; Dan Goldberg, 'Australian Jewish group slammed for urging boycott of West Bank settlement goods', *Haaretz*, 7 April 2013, www.haaretz.com/jewish-world/jewish-world-news/australian.

57   Jordy Silverstein, 'What are the possibilities of Jewish/Palestinian solidarity?', 24 June 2013, www.ajds.org.au/jewishpalestiniansolidarity/.

58   Peter Kohn, 'JCCV slams boycott decision', *Australian Jewish News*, 8 October 2010; Adam Kamien, 'AJDS gets rebuke for Israel boycott', *Australian Jewish News*, 7 June 2013, www.jewishnews.net.au/ajds-rebuked-over-israel-boycott/31087; Peter Wertheim, *Executive Council of Australian Jewry Annual Report* (2013), ECAJ, Sydney, 2013, pp.133–34.

59   Landy, *Jewish Identity and Palestinian Rights*, pp. 101, 162.

60   Paul Howes, Michael Leahy and Stuart Appelbaum, 'Unions move to overturn Israel boycott', *The Australian*, 21 May 2009, www.theaustralian.com.au/news/unions-move-to-overturn-israel-boycott/story-e6frg6n6-1225713790542; Leo Shanahan and Paul Maley, 'Israel boycott anger grows', *The Australian*, 16 April 2011, www.theaustralian.com.au/news/nation/israel-boycott-anger-grows/story-e6frg6nf-1226039947023.

61   Peter Kohn, 'Academics boycott BDS', *Australian Jewish News*, 21 October 2011; Nick Rowbotham, 'Union backs away from BDS motion', *New Matilda*, 6 June 2014, www.newmatilda.com/2014/06/06/union-backs-away-bds-motion.

62   Karkar, *Boycott Divestment Sanctions*, pp. 64–65; Patricia Karvelas, 'Unions to take Israel boycott plan to ACTU', *The Australian*, 15 October 2010, www.theaustralian.com.au/news/nation/unions-want-actu-to-endorse-protest-plan-against-israeli-settlements/story-e6frg6nf-1225938911111?nk=67f3d457195a1233d1de191da0fea1c0.

63   Antony Loewenstein, 'Australian unions, Paul Howes, BDS and loving Israel', *Crikey.com*, 11 November 2010, www.antony.wpmu.wud-web.com/2010/11/11/australian-unions-paul-howes-bds-and-loving-israel/.

64   David Cragg, *Report on Boycott Divestment Sanctions (of Israel) Conference*, Victorian Trades Hall Council Executive Council, Melbourne, 12 November 2010.

65   Victorian Trades Hall Council, 'Victorian Trades Hall supports BDS and condemn arrests of Max Brenner 19', 31 August 2011, www.boycottisrael19.wordpress.com/2011/08/31/victorian-trades-hall-supports-bds-and-condemn-arrests-of-max-brenner-19.

66   Eulalia Han and Halim Rane, *Making Australian foreign policy on Israel-Palestine*, Melbourne University Press, Melbourne, 2013, p. 144.

67   See comments of AFP's Moammar Mashni in Leo Shanahan,

'Greens boycott rebounds', *The Australian*, 19 April 2011, www.
theaustralian.com.au/news/features/greens-boycott-rebounds/story-
e6frg6z6-1226041184878.

68   Australians For Palestine, 'AFP refutes Jewish group's comparison
of BDS protests to Nazi anti-Semitic acts', 9 August 2011,
www.australiansforpalestine.com/wp-content/uploads/2011/06/
MR31AJDS-compares-BDS-to-Nai-anti-Semitism-9Aug11.pdf;
Karkar, *Boycott, Divestment Sanctions*, p. 39.

69   Chip Le Grand, 'Pro-Palestinian leader condemns violence
at Brenner boycott', *The Australian*, 16 August 2011, www.
theaustralian.com.au/national-affairs/pro-palestinian-
leader-condemns-violence-at-brenner-boycott/story-
fn59niix-1226115526356; Alex Bainbridge, 'BDS campaigners
meet in Adelaide for national conference', *Green Left Weekly*, 29
September 2012, www.greenleft.org.au/node/52390; P Wertheim &
A Ryvchin, *The Boycott, Divestment and Sanctions (BDS) Campaign
against Israel*, p. 8.

70   Imre Salusinzky, 'Palestinian consul rejects BDS violence', *The
Australian*, 26 October 2011, www.theaustralian.com.au/national-
affairs/palestinian-envoy-backs-bds-but-condemns-anti-israel-
violence/story-fn59niix-1226176664563&memtype=anonymous.

71   Barney Zwartz, 'Christians, Jews meet on boycott', *The Age*, 17
August 2010, www.theage.com.au/national/christians-jews-meet-
on-boycott-20100816-126y1.html.

72   Wertheim, *BDS suffers a defeat*, p. 6.

73   Ean Higgins, 'Libs to cut funding for anti-Israel activists',
The Australian, 25 May 2013, www.theaustralian.com.au/
national-affairs/libs-to-cut-funding-for-anti-israel-activists/story-
fn59niix-1226650231080.

74   Christian Kerr, 'Labor MP breaks ranks to table BDS petition
against apartheid Israel', *The Australian*, 29 October 2014.

75   Adam Kamien, 'Shorten: ALP opposes BDS', *Australian Jewish
News*, 31 October 2014.

4 Case study: BDS in Britain and North America

1   Ronnie Fraser, 'The Academic Boycott of Israel: Why Britain?',
Jerusalem Centre for Public Affairs, no. 36, 1 September 2005, www.
jcpa.org/phas/phas-36.htm.

2   Patrick Bateson et al, 'More pressure for Mid East peace',
Guardian, 6 April 2002, www.theguardian.com/world/2002/apr/06/
israel.guardianletters.

3   Hilary Rose & Steven Rose (2002) 'The choice is to do nothing or
try to bring about change', *Guardian*, 15 July.

4   Edward Alexander, *The State of the Jews: A Critical Appraisal*,
Transaction Publishers, New Brunswick, 2012, pp. 139–40.

5   Ned Curthoys, 'An argument for a moratorium', *Arena Magazine*,

no. 64, 2003; Audrea Lim, (ed.), *The Case for Sanctions against Israel*, Verso, London, 2012, pp. 219–21.

6   Philip Mendes, 'A case study of ethnic stereotyping: The campaign for an academic boycott of Israel', *Australian Journal of Jewish Studies*, vol. 20, 2006, pp. 143–45.

7   Mendes, 'A case study of ethnic stereotyping', p. 144; Author Unknown, 'Firing of Israeli Academics Fuels Debate over Use of Political Boycotts', *Jewish Telegraphic Agency*, 17 July 2002, www.jta.org/2002/07/17/archive/firing-of-israeli-academics-fuels-debate-over-use-of-political-boycotts.

8   See the relevant motion at www.parliament.uk/edm/print/2001-02/1590.

9   Mona Baker, 'Letters', *London Review of Books*, vol. 25, no. 17, 11 September 2003, www.lrb.co.uk/v25/n17/letters.

10   Mona Baker and Lawrence Davidson, 'In Defense of the Boycott of Israeli Academic Institutions', *Counterpunch*, 17 September 2003, www.counterpunch.org/2003/09/17/in-defense-of-the-boycott-of-israeli-academic-institutions/.

11   Luke Layfield, 'Oxford "appalled" as professor inflames boycott row', *Guardian*, 4 July 2003, www.theguardian.com/education/2003/jul/04/highereducation.internationaleducationnews.

12   Phil Baty, 'Oxford Rapped Over Wilkie', *Times Higher Educational Supplement*, 31 October 2003, www.timeshighereducation.co.uk/news/oxford-rapped-over-wilkie/184548.article.

13   See summary in P Mendes, 'A case study of ethnic stereotyping: The campaign for an academic boycott of Israel', *Australian Journal of Jewish Studies*, no. 20, 2006, pp. 143–44.

14   Mendes, 'A case study of ethnic stereotyping', p. 145.

15   David Hirsh, 'The Myth of Institutional Boycotts', 7 January 2014, *Inside Higher Ed*, www.insidehighered.com/views/2014/01/07/essay-real-meaning-institutional-boycotts.

16   The following paragraphs draw on Mendes, 'A case study of ethnic stereotyping', pp. 150–54.

17   'Israel universities – statement by AUT general secretary Sally Hunt', 22 April 2005, www.ucu.org.uk/index.cfm?articleid=1201.

18   'The University of Haifa Response to the AUT Decision', 1 May 2005, www.boycottnews.haifa.ac.il/html/html_eng/response_f.htm.

19   Polly Curtis and Will Woodward, 'Lecturers may boycott Israeli academics', *Guardian*, 5 April 2005, www.theguardian.com/uk/2005/apr/05/highereducation.internationaleducationnews; See www.aut.org.uk for the full motions.

20   'Israeli boycotts revoked - AUT statement', www.ucu.org.uk/index.cfm?articleid=1235; 'Academics Vote against Israeli Boycott,' *Guardian*, 26 May 2005, www.education.guardian.co.uk/higher/news/story/0,9830,1493083,00.html.

21   Omar Barghouti and Lisa Taraki, 'The AUT Boycott',
      Counterpunch, 1 June 2005, www.counterpunch.org/2005/06/01/
      the-aut-boycott/.

22   B Joffe-Walt, 'Lecturers back boycott of Israeli academics',
      Guardian, 30 May 2006.

23   Author Unknown, 'Lecturers call for Israel boycott', *BBC News*, 30
      May 2006, www.news.bbc.co.uk/2/hi/uk_news/education/5029086.
      stm.

24   'AFL-CIO President Richard Trumka Speaks Out Against
      Calls to Boycott Israel', 'Jewish Labor Committee', www.
      jewishlaborcommittee.org/2009/10/aflcio_president_richard_
      trumk_1.html.

25   'CUPE Ontario delegates support campaign against Israeli
      "apartheid wall"', 3 October 2014, www.web.archive.org/
      web/20060615191452/http://www.ontario.cupe.ca/www/
      background_on_resolution_50.

26   Kenyon Wallace, 'Ryan rebuked by national CUPE head', *The
      Star*, 14 January 2009, www.thestar.com/news/ontario/2009/01/14/
      ryan_rebuked_by_national_cupe_head.html.

27   Author Unknown, 'CUPE "intolerant" of Israel, Tories charge', *The
      Star*, 23 June 2009, www.thestar.com/news/canada/2009/02/23/
      cupe_intolerant_of_israel_tories_charge.html ; Michael Ignatieff,
      'Israel Apartheid Week and CUPE Ontario's anti-Israel posturing
      should be condemned', *National Post*, 5 March 2009, cited at
      www.spme.org/boycotts-divestments-sanctions-bds/boycotts-
      divestments-and-sanctions-bds-news/michael-ignatieff-israel-
      apartheid-week-and-cupe-ontarios-anti-israel-posturing-should-be-
      condemned/6513/; and see many of the responses listed at: www.
      zionismontheweb.org/academic_boycott/canadian_academic_
      boycott_of_israel/.

28   Wallace, 'Ryan rebuked by national CUPE head'; 'CUPE Ontario
      restates position on boycott of academic institutions', www.cupe.
      on.ca/d679/cupe-ontario-restates-position.

29   'CUPE 3902 Executive statement on the call for an academic
      boycott', cited at www.zionismontheweb.org/academic_boycott/
      canadian_academic_boycott_of_israel/CUPE_3902_executive_
      statement.htm; Paul Nahme et al, 'Sid Ryan, you have disgraced
      our union', *National Post*, 28 February 2009, www.labourwatch.
      com/docs/press/pdf/Sid_Ryan_you_have_disgraced_our_union.pdf.

30   Canadian Labour Congress, 'CLC Statement – Middle East, Israel
      & Gaza covering resolutions GR-12, GR-55, GR-85 and GR-86',
      www.canadianlabour.ca/convention/2011-convention/general-
      resolutions.

31   Fraser, 'The Academic Boycott of Israel'.

32   Ed O'Loughlin, 'Calls grow for boycott of Israel', *The Age*, 14 July
      2007, www.theage.com.au/news/world/calls-grow-for-boycott-of-

israel/2007/07/13/1183833772535.html ; the text of the letter can be seen at www.forward.com/articles/11344.

33 Ronnie Fraser, 'Trade Union and Other Boycotts of Israel in Great Britain', *Jerusalem Centre for Public Affairs*, no. 76, 1 December 2008, www.jcpa.org/article/trade-union-and-other-boycotts-of-israel-in-great-britain-and-ireland/.

34 See the example of the 'Dance Europe' magazine: www.ynetnews.com/articles/0,7340,L-3230909,00.html, in light of the claim on the BDS website: www.tiki-toki.com/timeline/entry/28282/BDS-Movementvars!panel=811997!

35 Avi Bar-Eli and Itai Trilnick, 'Not afraid to make money in Israel', *Haaretz*, 15 February 2012, www.haaretz.com/business/not-afraid-to-make-money-in-israel-1.412966.

36 The full text can be seen at www.presbyterianmission.org/ministries/global/resolution-israel-and-palestine-phased-selective-d/.

37 The full text can be seen at www.nimn.org/Resources/divestments/000454.php?section= .

38 'Action of the 217th General Assembly (2006) regarding Israel/Palestine' www.pcusa.org/site_media/media/uploads/global/pdf/ga217response.pdf.

39 Jon Haber, 'Divestment Meets its Waterloo in Somerville, Massachusetts', *Engage Journal*, Issue 1, 2006, www.engageonline.org.uk/journal/index.php?journal_id=5&article_id=21.

40 Author Unknown, 'Power of student action forces university to divest its holdings in major arms companies', *Wales Online*, www.walesonline.co.uk/news/wales-news/power-student-action-forces-university-2126263.

41 STUC, 'Supporting Palestinians Boycott Disinvestment & Sanctions Campaign Pack', www.stuc.org.uk/files/Palestine/BDS%20Document.pdf.

42 Author Unknown (Reproduction of Reuters article), 'Celtic fans urged to wave Palestinian flags at match against Tel Aviv club', *Haaretz*, 2 December 2009, www.haaretz.com/news/celtic-fans-urged-to-wave-palestinian-flags-at-match-against-tel-aviv-club-1.2958.

43 Marcus Dysch, 'Sussex Students' Union agrees Israel Boycott', *Jewish Chronicle*, 5 November 2009, www.thejc.com/campus/campus-news/21643/sussex-students-union-agrees-israel-boycott.

44 Hanna Ingber Win, 'Hampshire College Divests From Israel', *Huffington Post*, 15 March 2009, www.huffingtonpost.com/2009/02/12/hampshire-college-divests_n_166528.html; 'Hampshire College first in US to divest from Israel', *Electronic Intifada*, 12 February 2009, www.electronicintifada.net/content/hampshire-college-first-us-divest-israel/932.

45 'Correction of Misinformation Regarding Trustees' Actions on College Investments', 12 February 2009, www.hampshire.

edu/news/2009/02/12/correction-of-misinformation-regarding-trustees%C2%92-actions-on-college-investments.

46   'Hampshire College becomes first college in U.S. to divest from Israeli Occupation!', www.pacbi.org/etemplate.php?id=930.

47   'Statement on Israeli settlements in the Occupied Palestinian Territory', 2 September 2009, www.oikoumene.org/en/resources/documents/central-committee/2009/report-on-public-issues/statement-on-israeli-settlements-in-the-occupied-palestinian-territory; 'Methodist boycott of Israeli illegal settlements', www.methodist.org.uk/who-we-are/views-of-the-church/methodist-boycott-of-goods-from-illegal-israeli-settlements; Marcus Dysch and Simon Rocker, 'Fury as Methodists vote to boycott Israel', *Jewish Chronicle*, 1 July 2010, www.thejc.com/news/uk-news/33594/fury-methodists-vote-boycott-israel.

48   The following paragraphs draw on Philip Mendes, 'A case study of ethnic stereotyping: The campaign for an academic boycott of Israel', *Australian Journal of Jewish Studies*, vol. 20, 2006, pp. 150–58.

49   Gidley, *The politics of defining racism*, p. 4; D Hirsh (2013a) 'Does the UCU harbour hate? You decide', *The Jewish Chronicle*, 4 April.

50   D Hirsh (2013b) 'Fraser v UCU: tribunal finds no anti-Semitism at all', www.engageonline.wordpress.com/2013/04/18/fraser-v-ucu-tribunal, p. 3.

51   Hirsh, *Anti-Zionism and Antisemitism*, p.107.

52   Hirsh, 'Fraser v UCU'.

53   Eric Lee, 'World's unions reject boycotts, embrace Israeli-Palestinian cooperation', *Tulip Online*, 28 June 2010, www.tuliponline.org/?p=1930.

54   Maia Carter Hallward, *Transnational Activism and the Israeli-Palestinian Conflict*, Palgrave Macmillan, New York, 2013, pp. 66, 80–82.

55   Rolf Boone, 'Olympia Food Co-op boycotts Israel, pulls products', *The Olympian*, 21 July 2010, www.theolympian.com/2010/07/21/1310754_israel-cleaned-from-co-op-shelves.html.

56   Rolf Boone, Boycott evokes strong opinions', *The Olympian*, 24 July 2010, www.theolympian.com/2010/07/24/1314323/boycott-evokes-strong-opinions.html.

57   Olympia Food Co-op, 'Anti-Semitism and Progressive Movements?', 27 June 2010, www.olympiafoodcoop.blogspot.com.au/2010/07/anti-semitism-and-progressive-movements.html.

58   Jeremy Pawloski, 'Appeals Court upholds Olympia Food Co-op's boycott of Israeli goods', *The Olympian*, 7 April 2014, www.theolympian.com/2014/04/07/3074875/appeals-court-upholds-olympia.html.

59   Kirk Semple and Gersh Kuntzmann, 'Food Co-op Rejects Effort to Boycott Israeli-Made Products', *New York Times*, 27 March 2012,

www.nytimes.com/2012/03/28/nyregion/park-slope-food-co-op-
to-decide-on-boycott-vote.html?_r=0 ; Elizabeth Flock, 'The Park
Slope Food Coop boycott, explained', *Washington Post*, 28 March
2012,
www.washingtonpost.com/blogs/worldviews/post/the-park-slope-
food-co-op-boycott-explained/2012/03/28/gIQAlO2OgS_blog.htm.

60   Naomi Klein, 'Israel: Boycott, Divest, Sanction', *The Nation*, 26
January 2009, www.thenation.com/issue/january-26-2009?rel=hp_
currently; Naomi Klein, 'Enough. It's time for a boycott', *Guardian*,
10 January 2009, www.theguardian.com/commentisfree/2009/
jan/10/naomi-klein-boycott-israel.

61   Stephen Bates, 'Ian McEwan says he will accept Jerusalem prize',
Guardian, 20 January 2011, www.theguardian.com/books/2011/
jan/19/ian-mcewan-accept-jerusalem-prize; Robert Booth and
Harriet Sherwood, 'Noam Chomsky helped lobby Stephen
Hawking to stage Israel boycott', *Guardian*, 11 May 2013, www.
theguardian.com/world/2013/may/10/noam-chomsky-stephen-
hawking-israel-boycott.

62   Richard Pérez-Peña and Jodi Rudoren, 'Boycott by Academic
Group Is a Symbolic Sting to Israel', *New York Times*,
16 December 2013, www.nytimes.com/2013/12/17/education/
scholars-group-endorses-an-academic-boycott-of-israel.
html?pagewanted=all.

63   Associated Press, 'Palestinian university president comes out
against boycott of Israeli academics', *Haaretz*, 17 June 2006, www.
haaretz.com/news/palestinian-university-president-comes-out-
against-boycott-of-israeli-academics-1.190585.

64   Harriet Sherwood, 'Mahmoud Abbas accused of being traitor over
rejection of Israel boycott', *Guardian*, 22 December 2013, www.
theguardian.com/world/2013/dec/22/mahmoud-abbas-rejection-
israel-boycott.

65   'Noam Chomsky interviewed by Hicham Yezza', *Ceasefire*,
September 22, 2010, www.chomsky.info/interviews/20100922.htm;
Sherwood, 'Mahmoud Abbas accused of being traitor'; Ian Black,
'Israel boycott campaign risks backfiring, says Noam Chomsky',
Guardian, 3 July 2014, www.theguardian.com/world/2014/jul/02/
bds-boycott-campaign-israel-noam-chomsky.

66   Marcus Dysch, 'Finkelstein disowns "silly" Israel boycott', *Jewish
Chronicle*, 16 February 2012, www.thejc.com/news/uk-news/63662/
finkelstein-disowns-silly-israel-boycott.

67   'Protests disrupt Proms concert by Israel Philharmonic', *BBC News
UK*, 2 September 2011, www.bbc.co.uk/news/uk-14756736.

68   Author Unknown, 'UK's largest union backs boycott of Israel
despite Labor's calls to refrain', *Jerusalem Post*, www.jpost.com/
International/UKs-largest-union-backs-boycott-of-Israel-despite-
Labors-calls-to-refrain-361617.

69   Maya Shwayder, 134 members of US Congress denounce ASA's
      Israel boycott', *Jerusalem Post*, 19 January 2014, www.jpost.com/
      International/134-members-of-US-Congress-denounce-ASAs-
      Israel-boycott-338607; 'AAU Statement On Boycott Of Israeli
      Academic Institutions',
      20 December 2013, www.aau.edu/WorkArea/DownloadAsset.
      aspx?id=14859.

70   'What Does The Boycott Of Israeli Academic Institutions Mean
      For The ASA?' www.theasa.net/what_does_the_academic_boycott_
      mean_for_the_asa/.

71   Jonny Paul, 'Irish teachers union adopts full boycott of Israel',
      Jerusalem Post, 8 April 2013, www.jpost.com/Diplomacy-and-
      Politics/Irish-teachers-union-adopts-full-boycott-of-Israel-309133

72   See 'Palestine Motion 31' at www.teachers.org.uk/files/nut-final-
      agenda.pdf.

73   'Britain's National Union of Students approves BDS', *Times of
      Israel*, 4 August 2014, www.timesofisrael.com/britains-national-
      union-of-students-approves-bds/ixzz3FMuS20yr.

74   Warren Murray and Sam Jones, 'George Galloway refuses to
      debate with Israeli student at Oxford', *Guardian*, 21 February
      2013, www.theguardian.com/politics/2013/feb/21/george-
      galloway-debate-israeli-oxford; Author Unknown, 'Galloway under
      investigation over Israel remarks', *BBC News* UK, 7 August 2014,
      www.bbc.com/news/uk-politics-28687233.

75   Carter Hallward, *Transnational Activism*, p. 98.

76   Carter Hallward, *Transnational Activism*, p. 113, and see also
      'Landgraf announces no veto on divestment bill SB 160', www.
      dailycal.org/2013/04/23/landgraf-announces-no-veto-on-
      divestment-bill/.

77   Jonah Lowenfeld, ' Three UC student governments endorse BDS',
      Jewish Journal, 20 March 2013, www.jewishjournal.com/los_angeles/
      article/three_uc_student_governments_endorse_bds.

78   Steven Rosen, 'A European Boycott of Israel?', *Middle East
      Quarterly*, vol. 21, no. 2, Spring 2014, www.meforum.org/3747/
      europe-boycott-israel.

79   Tracy McVeigh and Harriet Sherwood 'Co-op boycotts exports from
      Israel's West Bank settlements', *Guardian*, 29 April 2012, www.
      theguardian.com/world/2012/apr/29/co-op-israel-west-bank-boycott.

80   Adam Kredo "How the boycott got boycotted', *Commentary*, 3
      January 2014, www.commentarymagazine.com/article/how-the-
      boycott-got-boycotted/ ; Scholars for Peace in the Middle East,
      BDS Monitor, 28 December 2013.

81   Scholars for Peace in the Middle East, *BDS Monitor*,
      28 February 2014; W Booth & R Eglash 'Pink Floyd hits out at
      Rolling Stones for playing in Israel', *Sydney Morning Herald*, 5 June
      2014.

82   Michael Posner, 'United Church of Canada approves Israeli
      settlement boycott', *Globe and Mail*, 17 August 2012, www.
      theglobeandmail.com/news/national/united-church-of-canada-
      approves-israeli-settlement-boycott/article4487724/.

83   Author Unknown, 'U.S. Presbyterians vote to divest from
      companies used by Israel in occupied territories', *Haaretz*, 21 June
      2014, www.haaretz.com/news/diplomacy-defense/1.600148.

84   Liel Leibovitz 'CUNY BDS Group Schedules Anti-Israel Vote for
      Shabbat', *Tablet Magazine*, 12 September 2014, www.tabletmag.
      com/scroll/184454/cuny-bds-group-schedules-anti-israel-vote-for-
      shabbat.

85   Martin Williams, 'Sainsbury's removes kosher food from shelves
      amid fears over protesters', *Guardian*, 18 August 2014, www.
      theguardian.com/business/2014/aug/17/sainsburys-removes-kosher-
      food-anti-israel-protesters.

86   Adam Withnall, 'Sports Direct security guard allegedly banned
      Jewish schoolboys and told them: "No Jews, no Jews"', *Independent*,
      16 September 2014, www.independent.co.uk/news/uk/home-news/
      sports-direct-security-guard-banned-jewish-schoolboys-and-told-
      them-no-jews-no-jews-9735919.html.

Conclusion: The progressive alternative to BDS

1   Michael Zakim, 'The Israel Boycott Is Working—to Prevent
     Peace', *The Chronicle of Higher Education*, 20 October 2014, www.
     chronicle.com/article/With-Friends-Like-These-/149393/?key=T2J2
     clcwYXhAMCtkNztGZmoGaXU/NUNxYnNLYiohblBXFg==.

2   David Remnick, 'The One-State Reality', *The New Yorker*,
     17 November 2013, www.newyorker.com/magazine/2014/11/17/
     one-state-reality.

3   Philip Mendes, 'Intervening in Israel', *Eureka Street*, vol. 23,
     no. 2, 4 February 2013, www.eurekastreet.com.au/article.
     aspx?aeid=34891.VGHB9PmUd8G.

4   Yossi Beilin, *The Path to Geneva: The quest for a permanent agreement,
     1996-2004*, RDV Books/Akashic Books, New York, 2004.

5   Yossi Beilin and Yasir Abed Rabbo, 'An accord to remember', *New
     York Times*, 1 December 2003.

6   Palestinian National Boycott Commmittee, 'The National
     Boycott Committee denounces the Palestinian Peace
     Coalition', 11 November 2014, www.alwatanvoice.com/arabic/
     news/2014/09/18/592752.html.

7   Board of Deputies of British Jews, *Boycott, Divestment and Sanctions
     of Israel: A response*, Board of Deputies of British Jews, London, pp.
     31–33.

8   David Hirsh, 'The Third Narrative Academic Advisory Council',
     Engage Online, 18 March 2014, www.engageonline.wordpress.
     com/2014/03/18/the-third-narrative.

Bibliography

David Aaronovitch, 'Why Israel will always be vilified', *Observer*, 24 April 2005.

Randa Abdel-Fattah, 'Who's afraid of BDS? Israel's assault on academic freedom', *ABC Religion and Ethics*, 31 October 2013.

Ali Abunimah, *One Country: A Bold Proposal to End the Israeli-Palestinian Impasse*, Metropolitan Books, New York, 2006.

Ali Abunimah, *The Battle for Justice in Palestine*, Haymarket Books, Chicago, 2014.

Academics for Palestine, *Academia against apartheid: The case for an academic boycott of Israel*, 19 February 2014.

Mira Adler-Gillies, 'BDS a last resort counter to Israeli exceptionalism', *The Drum*, 21 June 2011.

Amos Aikman and Leo Shanahan, 'Greens forced to back down on boycott', *The Australian*, 20 April 2011.

Pia Akerman and John Ferguson, 'Baillieu seeks to toughen protest laws', *The Australian*, 25 July 2012.

Nidal Al-Azza, 'Self-determination and the Right of Return: Interlinked and indivisible rights' in Rich Wiles (ed.), *Generation Palestine: Voices from the Boycott, Divestment and Sanctions Movement*, Pluto Press, London, 2013, pp. 72–78.

Edward Alexander, *The State of the Jews: A Critical Appraisal*, Transaction Publishers, New Brunswick, 2012.

Eric Alterman, 'Despicable Me', *The Nation*, 23 October 2013.

American Studies Association, 'What Does The Boycott Of Israeli Academic Institutions Mean For The ASA?', 2014, www.theasa. net/what_does_the_academic_boycott_mean_for_the_asa/.

Association of American Universities, 'AAU Statement on Boycott of Israeli Academic Institutions', 20 December 2013, www.aau.edu/ WorkArea/DownloadAsset.aspx?id=14859.

Association of University Teachers, 'Israeli boycotts revoked – AUT statement', 26 May 2005, www.ucu.org.uk/index. cfm?articleid=1235.

Australian Jewish Democratic Society, 'Statement on the JCCV's threatened disaffiliation', 6 May 2013, www.ajds.org.au/ajds-statement-on-the-jccvs-threatened-disaffiliation.

Australian Jewish Democratic Society Executive, 'AJDS statement update regarding BDS protests', 18 September 2011,

Boycotting Israel is Wrong

www.ajds.org.au/node/424.

Australian Senate, 'Israel: Boycotts', *Hansard Senate*, 24 March 2011.

Australians For Palestine, 'AFP refutes Jewish group's comparison of BDS protests to Nazi anti-Semitic acts', 9 August 2011, www.australiansforpalestine.com/wp-content/uploads/2011/06/MR31AJDS-compares-BDS-to-Nai-anti-Semitism-9Aug11.pdf.

Author Unknown, 'Academics Vote against Israeli Boycott', *Guardian*, 26 May 2005, http://education.guardian.co.uk/higher/news/story/0,9830,1493083,00.html.

Author Unknown, 'A campaign that is gathering weight', *The Economist*, 8 February 2014.

Author Unknown, 'Britain's National Union of Students approves BDS', *Times of Israel*, 4 August 2014, www.timesofisrael.com/britains-national-union-of-students-approves-bds/ixzz3FMuS20yr.

Author Unknown, 'Celtic fans urged to wave Palestinian flags at match against Tel Aviv club', *Haaretz*, 2 December 2009.

Author Unknown, 'CUPE "intolerant" of Israel, Tories charge', *The Star* (Canada), 23 June 2009.

Author Unknown, 'CUPE Ontario delegates support campaign against Israeli "apartheid wall"', 3 October 2014, www.web.archive.org/web/20060615191452/http://www.ontario.cupe.ca/www/background_on_resolution_50.

Author Unknown, 'Firing of Israeli Academics Fuels Debate over Use of Political Boycotts', *Jewish Telegraphic Agency*, 17 July 2002.

Author Unknown, 'Galloway under investigation over Israel remarks', *BBC News UK*, 7 August 2014.

Author Unknown, 'Hampshire College first in US to divest from Israel', *Electronic Intifada*, 12 February 2009.

Author Unknown, 'L'Chaim with Sodastream', *J-Wire*, 26 February 2014.

Author Unknown, 'Lecturers call for Israel boycott', *BBC News UK*, 30 May 2006.

Author Unknown, 'Palestinian university president comes out against boycott of Israeli academics', *Haaretz*, 17 June 2006.

Author Unknown, 'Power of student action forces university to divest its holdings in major arms companies', *Wales Online*, 27 January 2009.

Author Unknown, 'Protests disrupt Proms concert by Israel Philharmonic', *BBC News UK*, 2 September 2011.

Author Unknown, 'UK's largest union backs boycott of Israel despite Labor's calls to refrain', *Jerusalem Post*, 6 July 2014.

Author Unknown, 'U.S. Presbyterians vote to divest from companies used by Israel in occupied territories', *Haaretz*, 21 June 2014.

Uri Avnery, 'Taking apartheid apart', *Gush Shalom*, 26 October 2013.

Bibliography

Uri Avnery, 'Tutu's prayer', *Gush Shalom*, 31 August 2009.

Jed Babbin and Herbert London, *The BDS War Against Israel*, London Center for Policy Research, New York, 2014.

Alex Bainbridge, 'BDS campaigners meet in Adelaide for national conference', *Green Left Weekly*, 29 September 2012.

Abigail Bakan and Yameen Abu-Laban, 'Palestinian resistance and international solidarity: the BDS campaign', *Race & Class*, vol. 51, no. 1, 2009, pp. 29–54.

Mona Baker, 'Letters', *London Review of Books*, vol. 25, no. 17, 11 September 2003.

Mona Baker and Lawrence Davidson, 'In Defense of the Boycott of Israeli Academic Institutions', *Counterpunch*, 17 September 2003.

Anna Baltzer, *Witness in Palestine: Journal of a Jewish American Woman in the Occupied Territories*, Paradigm Publishers, Boulder, 2006.

Avi Bar-Eli and Itai Trilnick, 'Not afraid to make money in Israel', *Haaretz*, 15 February 2012.

Frank Barat, 'An Interview with Roger Waters', *Counterpunch*, Weekend Edition: 6–8 December 2013.

Mustafa Barghouti, 'Freedom in our lifetime', in Audrea Lim (ed.), *The Case for Sanctions against Israel*, Verso, London, 2012.

Omar Barghouti, *Boycott, Divestment, Sanctions: The Global Struggle for Palestinian Rights*, Haymarket Books, Chicago, 2011.

Omar Barghouti, 'Our South Africa Moment', in Moustafa Bayoumi (ed.), *Midnight on the Mavi Marmara: the attack on the Gaza Freedom Flotilla and How it Changed the Course of the Israel/Palestine Conflict*, Haymarket Books, Chicago, 2010.

Omar Barghouti, 'Setting the record straight on BDS', *New Matilda*, 2 May 2011.

Omar Barghouti, 'The cultural boycott: Israel vs South Africa', in Audrea Lim (ed.), *The Case for Sanctions against Israel*, Verso, London, 2011.

Omar Barghouti, 'The pianist of Palestine', *Counterpunch*, 29 November 2004.

Omar Barghouti, 'What comes next: A secular democratic state in historic Palestine – a promising land', *Mondoweiss*, 21 October 2013.

Omar Barghouti and Lisa Taraki, 'The AUT Boycott', *Counterpunch*, 1 June 2005.

Ramzyu Baroud, 'Palestine's global battle that must be won', in Rich Wiles (ed.), *Generation Palestine: Voices from the Boycott, Divestment and Sanctions Movement*, Pluto Press, London, 2013.

Stephen Bates, 'Ian McEwan says he will accept Jerusalem prize', *Guardian*, 20 January 2011.

Patrick Bateson et al, 'More pressure for Mid East peace', *Guardian*, 6 April 2002.

Phil Baty, 'Oxford Rapped Over Wilkie', *Times Higher Educational*

Supplement, 31 October 2003.

August Bebel, 'Assassinations and socialism', from a speech delivered by August Bebel, delivered at Berlin, November 2, 1898 (translated by Boris Reinstein), New York Labor News Company, New York, c. 1898.

Andy Beckett, 'It's water on stone – in the end the stone wears out', *Guardian*, 12 December 2002.

Yossi Beilin, *The Path to Geneva: The quest for a permanent agreement, 1996–2004*, RDV Books/Akashic Books, New York, 2004.

Yossi Beilin and Yasir Abed Rabbo, 'An accord to remember', *New York Times*, 1 December 2003.

Peter Beinart, *The Crisis of Zionism*, Henry Holt, New York, 2012.

Peter Beinart, 'The real problem with the American Studies Association's Boycott of Israel', *Daily Beast*, 17 December 2013.

Paul Berman, 'Something's changed: Bigotry in print. Crowds chant murder', in Ron Rosenbaum (ed.), *Those who forget the past: The question of Anti-Semitism*, Random House, New York, 2004.

Russell Berman, 'The goal of the boycott', *Los Angeles Review of Books*, 16 March 2014, pp. 1–11.

Ian Black, 'Israel boycott campaign risks backfiring, says Noam Chomsky', *Guardian*, 3 July 2014.

Board of Deputies of British Jews, *Boycott, Divestment and Sanctions of Israel: A response*, Board of Deputies of British Jews, London, 2013.

Yonah Jeremy Bob, 'Australian Professor: Law group sued me because BDS works', *Jerusalem Post*, 27 August 2013.

Rolf Boone, 'Boycott evokes strong opinions', *The Olympian*, 24 July 2010.

Rolf Boone, 'Olympia Food Co-op boycotts Israel, pulls products', *The Olympian*, 21 July 2010.

Robert Booth and Harriet Sherwood, 'Noam Chomsky helped lobby Stephen Hawking to stage Israel boycott', *Guardian*, 11 May 2013.

William Booth and Ruth Eglash, 'Pink Floyd hits out at Rolling Stones for playing in Israel', *Sydney Morning Herald*, 5 June 2014.

Alan Borowski et al, 'Boycott of Israel would penalise those most needed', *The Australian*, 29 May 2002.

Robert Bowker, *Palestinian Refugees: Mythology, identity and the search for peace*, Lynne Rienner Publishers, Boulder, 2003.

Harold Brackman, *Boycott Divestment Sanctions against Israel: An anti-Semitic, anti-peace poison pill*, Simon Wiesenthal Center, Los Angeles, 2013.

Julius Braunthal, *In search of the Millennium*, Victor Gollancz, London, 1945.

Julius Braunthal, *The Significance of Israeli Socialism and the Arab-Israeli Dispute*, Lincolns-Prager, London, 1958.

British Labour Party Executive, 'A policy for Palestine', *Extract from the*

Bibliography

'International Post-war Settlement' Report submitted to the 43rd Annual Conference, 11–15 December 1944, London.

Kim Bullimore, 'BDS and the struggle for a free Palestine', in Antony Loewenstein and Jeff Sparrow (eds), *Left Turn: Political essays for the new left*, Melbourne University Press, Melbourne, 2012.

Judith Butler, 'Israel/Palestine and the paradoxes of academic freedom', *Radical Philosophy*, vol. 135, January/February 2006, pp. 8–17.

Fiona Byrne, 'Taking local action on international issues', *The Drum Unleashed*, 13 January 2011.

Canadian Labour Congress, 'CLC Statement – Middle East, Israel & Gaza covering resolutions GR-12, GR-55, GR-85 and GR-86', *Report of the Canadian Labour Congress's 26th Constituional Convention*.

Centre for Peace and Conflict Studies, 2009 *Annual Report*, University of Sydney, Sydney.

Naomi Chazan, 'BDS, the boycott law and Israel's democracy', *Bitterlemons*, 21 July 2011, Edition 22.

Naomi Chazan, 'The quest for a two-state solution', *The Drum*, 17 June 2011.

Noam Chomsky, 'On Israel-Palestine and BDS', *The Nation*, 2 July 2014.

Roger Cohen, 'Zero Dark Zero', *New York Times*, 28 February 2013.

Steve Cohen, 'I would hate myself in the morning', *Engage Online*, 29 May 2006.

Christine Collette, 'The utopian visions of Labour Zionism, British Labour, and the Labour and Socialist International in the 1930s', in Christine Collette & Stephen Bird (eds), *Jews, Labour and the Left, 1918–48*, Ashgate, Aldershot, 2000.

David Cragg, *Report on Boycott Divestment Sanctions (of Israel) Conference*, Victorian Trades Hall Council Executive Council, Melbourne, 12 November 2010.

Stan Crooke, 'Boycott Apartheid Israel', in August Grabski (ed.), *Rebels Against Zion: Studies on the Jewish Left Anti-Zionism*, Jewish Institute of History, Warsaw, 2011.

Stan Crooke, 'The Stalinist roots of left anti-Semitism', *Workers' Liberty*, no. 10, May 1988, pp. 30–37.

RHS Crossman and Michael Foot, *A Palestine Munich?*, Victor Gollancz, London, 1946.

Ned Curthoys, 'An argument for a moratorium', *Arena Magazine*, no. 64, 2003, pp. 26–28.

Ned Curthoys, John Docker and Antony Loewenstein, 'Palestine's Ghandi – Omar Barghouti, BDS and int'l [sic] law', *Overland Blog*, 31 May 2011.

Polly Curtis, 'Lecturers vote for Israeli boycott', *Guardian*, 22 April 2005.

Polly Curtis, 'Suspension not enough for Oxford don, say students', *Guardian*, 28 October 2003.

Polly Curtis and Will Woodward, 'Lecturers may boycott Israeli academics', *Guardian*, 5 April 2005.

Michael Danby, 'Anti-Israel protests don't deserve support', *Herald Sun*, 27 July 2012.

John Docker, 'Thirteen untimely meditations', *Arena Magazine*, no. 55, 2001, pp. 9–11.

John Docker and Ghassan Hage, 'Boycott just the way to rap Israel', *The Australian*, 22 May 2002.

Mark Dodd and Sid Maher, 'Bob Brown told to rein in anti-Israel senator Lee Rhiannon', *The Australian*, 1 April 2011.

Paul Duffill, 'Establishing the facts about the boycott of Israeli academic institutions', *The Conversation*, 15 January 2013.

Paul Duffill and Gabriella Scoff, 'Growing Jewish support for boycott and the changing landscape of the BDS debate', *Mondoweiss*, 17 June 2014.

Nick Dyrenfurth, 'Boycotting Israel another impediment to peace', *The Saturday Paper*, 19 April 2014.

Marcus Dysch, 'Finkelstein disowns "silly" Israel boycott', *Jewish Chronicle*, 16 February 2012.

Marcus Dysch, 'Sussex Students' Union agrees Israel Boycott', *Jewish Chronicle*, 5 November 2009.

Marcus Dysch and Simon Rocker, 'Fury as Methodists vote to boycott Israel', *Jewish Chronicle*, 1 July 2010.

June Edmunds, *The Left and Israel: Party-Policy Change and Internal Democracy*, Macmillan, London, 2000.

Yehuda Eloni, 'The Zionist Movement and the German Social Democratic Party, 1897–1918', *Studies in Zionism*, vol. 5, no. 2, 1984, pp. 181–99.

Engage, 'Why boycott Israeli Universities? A response to Bricup', *Engage Online*, May 2007.

Noura Erakat, 'BDS in the USA, 2001–2010', in Audrea Lim (ed.), *The Case for Sanctions against Israel*, Verso, London, 2012.

Noura Erakat, 'Structural violence on trial: BDS and the movement to resist erasure', *Los Angeles Review of Books*, 16 March 2014, pp. 1–9.

Executive Council of Australian Jewry, 'ECAJ urges restraint in rhetoric', 14 September 2011, www.ecaj.org.au/2011/ecaj-urges-restraint-in-rhetoric/.

Robert Fine, 'Address to Leeds University BDS debate', *Engage Online*, 21 March 2014.

Norman Finkelstein, 'Norman Finkelstein on BDS', *YouTube*, 15 February 2012.

Norman Finkelstein, 'What comes next: If the goal is to change U.S. policy, American Jewish opinion can't be ignored', *Mondoweiss*, 22

October 2013.

Elizabeth Flock, 'The Park Slope Food Coop boycott, explained', *Washington Post*, 28 March 2012.

Liz Ford, 'Boycotts self-defeating, Israel conference told', *Guardian*, 26 January 2006.

Jonathan Frankel, 'The Soviet regime and Anti-Zionism: An Analysis', in Ezra Mendelsohn (ed.), *Essential Papers on Jews and the Left*, New York University Press, New York, 1997.

Matthew Franklin and Amos Aikman, 'Anti-Israel stance focus of Greens review', *The Australian*, 28 March 2011.

Ronnie Fraser, 'The Academic Boycott of Israel: Why Britain?', *Jerusalem Centre for Public Affairs*, no. 36, 1 September 2005.

Ronnie Fraser, 'Trade Union and Other Boycotts of Israel in Great Britain', *Jerusalem Centre for Public Affairs*, no. 76, 1 December 2008.

Jonathan Freedland, 'Firing on our friends', *Guardian*, 8 July 2002.

Saul Friedlander, *Nazi Germany and the Jews: Volume 1: The Years of Persecution: 1933–1939*, Harper Collins, New York, 1997.

Shlomo Gazit, 'Many instances of discrimination', *Bitterlemons*, no. 8, 2012.

Manfred Gerstenfeld, *Academics against Israel and the Jews*, Jerusalem Center for Public Affairs, Jerusalem, 2007.

Ben Gidley, 'The politics of defining racism: The case of Anti-Semitism in the University and College Union', *Dissent*, 26 May 2011.

Daryl Glaser, 'Zionism and Apartheid: a moral comparison', *Ethnic and Racial Studies*, vol. 26, no. 3, 2003, pp. 403–421.

Dan Goldberg, 'Australian court case fires up BDS campaign against Israel', *Haaretz*, 30 April 2013.

Dan Goldberg, 'Australian Jewish group slammed for urging boycott of West Bank settlement goods', *Haaretz*, 7 April 2013.

Jeffrey Goldberg, 'Kerry's Israel boycott talk will backfire', *Bloomberg*, 6 February 2014.

Yoel Goldman, 'Abbas: Don't boycott Israel', *Times of Israel*, 13 December 2013.

Yoel Goldman, 'Universities quit US academic body over Israel boycott', *Times of Israel*, 19 December 2013.

Gershom Gorenberg, *The Unmaking of Israel*, HarperCollins, New York, 2011.

Yosef Gorny, *Converging Alternatives: The Bund and the Zionist Labor Movement, 1897–1985*, State University of New York Press, New York, 2006.

David Graham and Jonathan Boyd, *Committed, concerned and conciliatory: the attitudes of Jews in Britain towards Israel*, Institute for Jewish Policy Research, London, 2010.

Andrei Gromyko, *Address to United Nations General Assembly*, 1st

Special Session, 77th Plenary Meeting, 14 May 1947, vol. 1, pp. 127–35.

Sara Grossman, 'Landgraf announces no veto on divestment bill SB 160', *The Daily Californian*, 23 April 2013.

Jon Haber, 'Divestment Meets its Waterloo in Somerville, Massachusetts', *Engage Journal*, Issue 1, January 2006.

Ghassan Hage, *Against Paranoid Nationalism*, Pluto Press, Sydney, 2002.

Maia Carter Hallward, *Transnational Activism and the Israeli-Palestinian Conflict*, Palgrave Macmillan, New York, 2013.

Eulalia Han and Halim Rane, *Making Australian foreign policy on Israel-Palestine*, Melbourne University Press, Melbourne, 2013.

Peter Hartcher, 'What am I, chopped liver? How Rudd dived into Schmooze mode', *Sydney Morning Herald*, 22 June 2010.

Elias Heifetz, *The Slaughter of the Jews in the Ukraine in 1919*, Thomas Seltzer, New York, 1921.

Marjorie Heins, 'Rethinking Academic Boycotts', *AAUP Journal of Academic Freedom*, vol. 4, 2013, pp. 1–12.

Julie Henry, 'Outrage as Oxford bans student for being Israeli', *Daily Telegraph*, 29 June 2003.

Jacob Hen-Tov, *The Comintern and Zionism in Palestine*, PhD thesis, Brandeis University, 1969.

Ean Higgins, 'BDS vindicated by Israeli activists loss', *The Australian*, 16 July 2014.

Ean Higgins, 'Israel sanctions backers miffed', *The Australian*, 11 June 2014.

Ean Higgins, 'Libs to cut funding for anti-Israel activists', *The Australian*, 25 May 2013.

Ean Higgins and Christian Kerr, 'Jihad Sheila link to anti-Jewish posts', *The Australian*, 3 May 2013.

Nadia Hijab, 'For human rights advocates, supporting BDS is a no-brainer', *Bitterlemons*, edition 22, 22 July 2011.

David Hirsh, *Anti-Zionism and Antisemitism: Cosmopolitan Reflections*, Yale Initiative for the Interdisciplinary Study of Antisemitism Occasional Papers, New Haven, 2007.

David Hirsh, 'Civility in contemporary debates about anti-Semitism,' *Jewish Quarterly*, vol. 61, no.1, Spring 2014, pp. 38–39.

David Hirsh, 'Does the UCU harbour hate? You decide', *The Jewish Chronicle*, 4 April 2013.

David Hirsh, 'Fraser v UCU: tribunal finds no anti-Semitism at all', *Engage Online*, 18 April 2013.

David Hirsh, 'The American Studies Association boycott resolution, academic freedom and the myth of the institutional boycott', *Engage Online*, 7 January 2014.

David Hirsh, 'The Myth of Institutional Boycotts', *Inside Higher Ed*, 7 January 2014.

Bibliography

David Hirsh, 'The Third Narrative Academic Advisory Council', *Engage Online*, 18 March 2014.

Christopher Hitchens, 'Anti-Semitism: The Socialism of Fools', *New Statesman*, 20 June 1980, p. 928.

Simon Holt, 'Marrickville's boycott of Israel blasted by PM Julia Gillard', *Inner West Courier*, 11 May 2011.

Paul Howes, 'Radicalism may force Greens to change tunes', *Sunday Telegraph*, 3 April 2011.

Paul Howes, Michael Leahy and Stuart Appelbaum, 'Unions move overturn Israel boycott', *The Australian*, 21 May 2009.

Justin Huggler and Josie Ensor, 'Anti-Semitism on the march: Europe braces for violence', *The Telegraph* (London), 26 July 2014.

Sally Hunt, 'Israel universities – statement by AUT general secretary Sally Hunt', 22 April 2005, www.ucu.org.uk/index. cfm?articleid=1201.

Tom Hyland, 'Row over Israeli chocolate leaves a bitter taste', *The Age*, 18 September 2011.

Michael Ignatieff, 'Israel Apartheid Week and CUPE Ontario's anti-Israel posturing should be condemned', *National Post*, 5 March 2009.

Hanna Ingber Win, 'Hampshire College Divests From Israel', *Huffington Post*, 15 March 2009.

Israel Central Bureau of Statistics, *Selected data on the occasion of Jerusalem Day*, 2014, www1.cbs.gov.il/www/ hodaot2013n/11_13_119e.pdf.

Timna Jacks, 'Israel supporters take to Melbourne streets', *Australian Jewish News*, 9 September 2011.

Jack Jacobs, *Bundist Anti-Zionism in Interwar Poland*, Wallstein Verlag, Sonderdruck, 2005.

Andrew Jakubowicz, 'Anatomy of a boycott', *Sydney Morning Herald*, 8 February 2003.

Andrew Jakubowicz, 'Civility and terror in academic life: The Israeli academic boycotts', *Borderlands*, vol. 2, no. 3, 2003, pp. 1–10.

Marc Jarblum, *The Socialist International and Zionism*, Poale Zion of America, New York, 1933.

Jewish Labor Committee, 'AFL-CIO President Richard Trumka Speaks Out Against Calls to Boycott Israel', www.jewishlaborcommittee. org/2009/10/aflcio_president_richard_trumk_1.html.

Jewish Telegraphic Agency, 'Dutch pro-Palestine group defends "Jews control Internet" article', *Haaretz*, 10 February 2014.

Benjamin Joffe-Walt, 'Lecturers back boycott of Israeli academics', *Guardian*, 30 May 2006.

Alan Johnson, 'BDS bullies at Galway University', *Times of Israel*, 10 March 2014.

Alan Johnson, 'Bob Crow: a two states for two peoples trade unionist', *Left Foot Forward*, 11 March 2014.

Alan Johnson, *The Apartheid Smear*, Britain/Israel Communications & Research Centre, London, 2014.

Jonathan Judaken, *Jean-Paul Sartre and the Jewish Question*, University of Nebraska Press, Lincoln, 2006.

Anthony Julius, *Trials of the Diaspora*, Oxford University Press, Oxford, 2010.

Matthew Kalman, 'Palestinians divided over boycott of Israeli universities', *New York Times*, 19 January 2014.

Adam Kamien, 'AJDS gets rebuke for Israel boycott', *Australian Jewish News*, 7 June 2013.

Adam Kamien, 'Shorten: ALP opposes BDS', *Australian Jewish News*, 31 October 2014.

Carolyn Karcher, 'Why I voted for an academic boycott of Israel', *Los Angeles Times*, 27 December 2013.

Sonja Karkar, *Boycott Divestment Sanctions: A global campaign to end Israeli Apartheid*, Australians for Palestine, Melbourne, 2010.

Joshua M Karlip, *The tragedy of a generation: The rise and fall of Jewish nationalism in Eastern Europe*, Harvard University Press, Cambridge, 2013.

Ghada Karmi, 'The weapon of the weak', *Bitterlemons*, no. 26, pp. 3–4.

Patricia Karvelas, 'Unions to take Israel boycott plan to ACTU', *The Australian*, 15 October 2010.

Paul Kelemen, *The British Left and Zionism: History of a divorce*, Manchester University Press, Manchester, 2012.

Ari Y Kelman, 'Engage, Don't Boycott: An open letter to the American Studies Association', *The Nation*, 13 December 2013.

Gael Kennedy and Janet Kossy, 'Councils can help Mid-East peace', *National Times*, 19 April 2011.

Andrew Kent, 'Evaluating the Palestinians' Claimed Right of Return', *University of Pennsylvania Journal of International Law*, no. 34, 2012, pp. 149–236.

Christian Kerr, 'Anti-Israel lobby defiant on uni rally', *The Australian*, 28 August 2013.

Christian Kerr, 'Centre chief rebuked over snub to Israeli', *The Australian*, 8 December 2012.

Christian Kerr, 'Labor MP breaks ranks to table BDS petition against apartheid Israel', *The Australian*, 29 October 2014.

Christian Kerr, 'PM denounces activists as anti-Israel protest turns anti-Semitic', *The Australian*, 30 April 2013.

Christian Kerr, 'Protests lack link to Israel: BDS fan', *The Australian*, 2 May 2013.

Christian Kerr, 'Sydney University rejects call for Israel boycott', *The Australian*, 10 May 2013.

Christian Kerr, 'Uni peace centre rebuffs Israeli civics teacher', *The Australian*, 6 December 2012.

Bibliography

Baruch Kimmerling, 'The meaning of academic boycott', *Borderlands*, vol. 2, no. 3, 2003, pp. 1–10.

Baruch Kimmerling, 'The meaning of academic boycott', *Z Net*, 26 April 2005.

Martin Luther King, 'Open letter to President Johnson', *New York Times*, 28 May 1967.

Doug Kirsner, Ari Suss and Geoffrey Winn, 'Hot chocolate a cure for those who ignore history', *The Punch*, 23 August 2011.

Naomi Klein, 'Enough. It's time for a boycott', *Guardian*, 10 January 2009.

Naomi Klein, 'Israel: Boycott, Divest, Sanction', *The Nation*, 26 January 2009.

Peter Kohn, 'Academics boycott BDS', *Australian Jewish News*, 21 October 2011.

Peter Kohn, 'BDS supporters cancel synagogue demonstration', *Australian Jewish News*, 17 February 2012.

Peter Kohn, 'JCCV slams boycott decision', *Australian Jewish News*, 8 October 2010.

Adam Kredo, 'How the boycott got boycotted', *Commentary*, 3 January 2014.

Adam Kredo, 'Palestinian activists violently threaten pro-Israel students', *The Washington Free Beacon*, 21 March 2014.

Dauod Kuttab, 'At Mandela funeral, Abbas says he opposes boycott of Israel', *Al Monitor*, 13 December 2013.

Daoud Kuttab, 'The problems with boycotts', *Bitterlemons*, no. 16, 2005, pp. 4–6.

David Landy, *Jewish identity and Palestinian rights: Diaspora Jewish opposition to Israel*, Zed Books, London, 2011.

Shalom Lappin, 'Why I resigned from the AUT', 28 April 2005, www.normblog.typepad.com/normblog/2005/04/why_i_resigned_.html.

Luke Layfield, 'Oxford "appalled" as professor inflames boycott row', *Guardian*, 4 July 2003.

Alon Lee, 'Academics fight back on Israel boycott bid', *Australian Jewish News*, 31 May 2002.

Eric Lee, 'Palestinians tell British union: Don't sever ties with the Histadrut', *Tulip Online*, 18 April 2011.

Eric Lee, 'World's unions reject boycotts, embrace Israeli-Palestinian cooperation', *Tulip Online*, 28 June 2010.

Chip Le Grand, 'Pro-Palestinian leader condemns violence at Brenner boycott', *The Australian*, 16 August 2011.

Liel Leibovitz 'CUNY BDS Group Schedules Anti-Israel Vote for Shabbat', *Tablet Magazine*, 12 September 2014.

Michael Lerner, 'Nelson Mandela: A Jewish perspective', *Tikkun Magazine online*, 7 December 2013.

Audrea Lim (ed.), *The Case for Sanctions against Israel*, Verso, London, 2012.

Seymour Martin Lipset, 'The Return of Anti-Semitism as a Political Force', in Irving Howe and Carl Gershman (eds), *Israel, The Arabs and the Middle East*, Bantam Books, New York, 1972.

David Lloyd, 'What threatens Israel most? Democracy', *Los Angeles Review of Books*, 16 March 2014, pp. 1–7.

Antony Loewenstein, 'Australian unions, Paul Howes, BDS and loving Israel', *Crikey.com*, 11 November 2010.

Antony Loewenstein, 'Marrickville madness over BDS but Palestinian rights aren't forgotten', www.antonyloewenstein.com/2011/04/20/marrickville-madness-over-bds-but-palestine-rights-arent-forgotten/.

Antony Loewenstein, 'To support the boycott, divestment and sanctions movement is not antisemitic', *Guardian*, 8 November 2013.

Antony Loewenstein, 'Why boycotting Israel matters', *The Drum*, 18 December 2012.

Jonah Lowenfeld, ' Three UC student governments endorse BDS', *Jewish Journal*, 20 March 2013.

Jake Lynch, 'Can the centre hold? Prospects for mobilizing media activism around public service broadcasting using peace journalism', in Ibrahim Seaga Shaw, Jake Lynch and Robert A Hackett (eds), *Expanding peace journalism: comparative and critical approaches*, Sydney University Press, Sydney, 2010, pp. 287–316.

Jake Lynch, *Debates in Peace Journalism*, Sydney University Press, Sydney, 2008.

Jake Lynch, 'Letter to Professor Michael Spence, Vice-Chancellor The University of Sydney', 3 June 2009.

Jake Lynch, 'Toeing the Lobby Line', *New Matilda*, 8 February 2011.

Graeme McCulloch, 'Editorial note', *NTEU Advocate*, no. 6, November 2012.

Moshe Machover, *Israelis and Palestinians*, Haymarket Books, Chicago, 2012.

Tracy McVeigh and Harriet Sherwood 'Co-op boycotts exports from Israel's West Bank settlements', *Guardian*, 29 April 2012.

Shlomo Maital, 'Dissecting BDS', *Jerusalem Report*, vol. 24, no. 26, 7 April 2014, pp. 32–36.

Paul Maley, 'Council boycott of Israel self-indulgent', *The Australian*, 13 January 2011.

Andrew Markus, Nicky Jacobs and Tanya Aronov, *2008-9 Jewish Population Survey*, Monash University Australian Centre for Jewish Civilisation, Melbourne, 2008.

Marrickville Council, *Minutes of Council Meeting*, 19 April 2011.

Philip Mendes, 'A case study of ethnic stereotyping: The campaign for an academic boycott of Israel', *Australian Journal of Jewish Studies*, no. 20, 2006, pp. 141–68.

Philip Mendes, 'Advocating peace or promoting conflict and

discrimination? The strange case of the Centre for Peace and Conflict Studies', *Galus Australis*, 23 March 2011.

Philip Mendes, 'Australian Jewish Dissent on Israel: A History of the Australian Jewish Democratic Society (Part 1)', *Australian Jewish Historical Society Journal*, November 1999, pp. 117–38.

Philip Mendes, 'Denying the Jewish Experience of Oppression: the Jewish anti-Zionism of John Docker', *Australian Journal of Jewish Studies*, no. 17, 2003, pp. 112–30.

Philip Mendes, 'Intervening in Israel', *Eureka Street*, vol. 23, no. 2, 4 February 2013.

Philip Mendes, 'Israel's Camp David peace proposal: generous offer or sham?', *Australian Quarterly*, Vol. 76, no.1, January–February 2004, pp. 14–17.

Philip Mendes, *Jews and the Left: The rise and fall of a political alliance*, Palgrave Macmillan, London, 2014.

Philip Mendes, 'The Australian Greens and the Israeli-Palestinian conflict', in Dashiel Lawrence and Shahar Burla (eds), *Australia-Israel: A diasporic, cultural and political relationship*, Sussex Academic Press, Brighton, 2015. (In Press.)

Philip Mendes, 'The Australian Greens: Taking Sides on the Israeli/Palestinian Conflict', *B'nai B'rith Anti-Defamation Commission Special Report*, No. 22, September 2004.

Philip Mendes, 'The Australian Left's support for the creation of the State of Israel, 1947–48', *Labour History*, no. 97, 2009, pp. 137–48.

Philip Mendes, *The New Left, the Jews and the Vietnam War 1965–72*, Lazare Press, Melbourne, 1993.

Daniel Meyerowitz-Katz, 'Incitement watch: BDS harasses synagogue-goers in the US while Arabic media see Jewish plots everywhere', 13 June 2013, www.aijac.org.au/news/article/incitement-watch-bds-group-harasses-synagogue-go.

Daniel Meyerowitz-Katz, 'Sue me Jew: Horrific hate-speech by Australian students on anti-Israel Facebook page', 29 April 2013, www.aijac.org.au/news/article/sue-me-jew-horrific-hate-speech-by-australian-st.

Cahal Milmo, 'Jewish academic Moty Crista sues Unison for racial discrimination', *Independent*, 12 September 2013.

Ahmed Moor, 'BDS is a long term project with radically transformative potential', *Mondoweiss*, 22 April 2010.

Rick Morton, 'Diplomacy better than Israel boycott: Rudd', *The Australian*, 17 January 2013.

Bill V Mullen, 'Palestine, Boycott and Academic Freedom: A reassessment introduction', *AAUP Journal of Academic Freedom*, vol. 4, 2013.

Warren Murray and Sam Jones, 'George Galloway refuses to debate with Israeli student at Oxford', *Guardian*, 21 February 2013.

Ali Mustafa, 'Boycotts work – an interview with Omar Barghouti',

Electronic Intifada, 31 May 2009.

David Myers, 'Why I oppose a boycott, mostly', *Los Angeles Review of Books*, 16 March 2014, pp. 1–8.

Paul Nahme et al, 'Sid Ryan, you have disgraced our union', *National Post*, 28 February 2009.

Gareth Narunsky, 'New Greens leader: BDS is behind us', *Australian Jewish News*, 20 April 2012.

Sally Neighbour, 'Divided we fall', *The Monthly*, February 2012, pp. 21–28.

Cary Nelson, 'The new assault on Israeli academia (and us)', *Fathom*, 22 September 2014.

Cary Nelson, 'The problem with Judith Butler: The political philosophy of the movement to boycott Israel', *Los Angeles Review of Books*, 16 March 2014, pp. 1–21.

Cary Nelson and Gabriel Noah Brahm, *The Case Against Academic Boycotts of Israel*, Wayne State University Press, Chicago, 2015.

Donna Nevel, 'Boycott, Divestment and Sanctions (BDS) and the American Jewish Community', *Tikkun Daily*, 7 March 2014.

David Newman, 'The ultimatum set by the University of Johannesburg for Ben Gurion University', *Jerusalem Post*, 4 October 2010.

Sean Nicholls and Jo Tovey, 'Anti-Israel boycott opens fresh split in Greens', *Sydney Morning Herald*, 9 September 2011.

Stephen H Norwood, *Antisemitism and the American Far Left*, Cambridge University Press, New York, 2013.

Ed O'Loughlin, 'Calls grow for boycott of Israel', *The Age*, 14 July 2007.

Olympia Food Co-op, 'Anti-Semitism and Progressive Movements?', 27 June 2010, www.olympiafoodcoop.blogspot.com.au/2010/07/anti-semitism-and-progressive-movements.html.

Ontario section of the Canadian Union of Public Employees, 'CUPE Ontario restates position on boycott of academic institutions', www.cupe.on.ca/d679/cupe-ontario-restates-position

Ontario section of the Canadian Union of Public Employees, 'CUPE 3902 Executive statement on the call for an academic boycott', cited at www.zionismontheweb.org/academic_boycott/canadian_academic_boycott_of_israel/CUPE_3902_executive_statement.htm.

Emanuele Ottolenghi, 'Present-day Antisemitism and the centrality of the Jewish alibi', in Alvin H Rosenfeld (ed.), *Resurgent Antisemitism*, Indiana University Press, Bloomington, 2013, pp. 424–66.

Palestinian BDS National Committee, 'BDS movement position on boycott of individuals', 21 February 2013, www.bdsmovement.net/2013/bds-movement-position-on-boycott-of-individuals-10679.

Palestinian BDS National Committee, 'BNC condemns repression of BDS activism in Australia', 17 August 2011, www.bdsmovement.net/2011/bnc-condemns-repression-of-bds-activism-in-australia-7866.

Bibliography

Palestinian Campaign for the Academic and Cultural Boycott of Israel, 'Guidelines for the International Academic Boycott of Israel', revised July 2014, www.pacbi.org/etemplate.php?id=1108.

Palestinian National Boycott Commmittee, 'The National Boycott Committee denounces the Palestinian Peace Coalition', 11 November 2014, www.alwatanvoice.com/arabic/news/2014/09/18/592752.html.

Ilan Pappe, 'Colonialism, the peace process and the academic boycott', in Rich Wiles (ed.), *Generation Palestine*, Pluto Press, London, 2013.

Jack Passaris, 'Letter to Marrickville Council Mayor Fiona Byrne' in Peter Wertheim, *BDS suffers a defeat in Australia: The Marricville Council Controversy*, Executive Council of Australian Jewry, Sydney, 2011, p. 28.

Graeme Paton, 'Lecturers consider Israel boycott', *Daily Telegraph* (London), 2 June 2007.

Jonny Paul, 'Irish teachers union adopts full boycott of Israel', *Jerusalem Post*, 8 April 2013.

Jeremy Pawloski, 'Appeals Court upholds Olympia Food Co-op's boycott of Israeli goods', *The Olympian*, 7 April 2014.

Danielle Peled, 'It's hard to be an anti-Zionist', *Jerusalem Report*, 16 (3), 30 May 2005, pp. 25–26.

Ilan Peleg and Dov Waxman, *Israel's Palestinians: The conflict within*, Cambridge University Press, Cambridge, 2011.

Richard Pérez-Peña and Jodi Rudoren, 'Boycott by Academic Group Is a Symbolic Sting to Israel', *New York Times*, 16 December 2013.

Louise Perry and Megan Saunders, 'Vote on Ashrawi award not split', *The Australian*, 24 October 2003.

Verashni Pillay, 'Shoot the Jew song slammed', *Mail and Guardian*, 2 September 2013.

Benjamin Pinkus and Jonathan Frankel, *The Soviet Government and the Jews 1948-1967: A documented study*, Cambridge University Press, Cambridge, 1984.

Johann Pollak, 'Der politische Zionismus', *Die Neue Zeit*, vol. 16, no. 1, 1897–98, pp. 598–600.

Benjamin Pogrund, 'Boycotts only harden Israeli opinion', *Guardian*, 24 August 2009.

Benjamin Pogrund, *Drawing Fire: Investigating The Accusations of Apartheid in Israel*, Rowman and Littlefield, Lanham, 2014.

Michael Posner, 'United Church of Canada approves Israeli settlement boycott', *Globe and Mail*, 17 August 2012.

Ronald Radosh and Allis Radosh, 'Righteous among the editors: When the Left loved Israel', *World Affairs*, vol. 171, no. 1, 2008, pp. 65–75.

Alan Ramsey, 'Here's Lucy, caving in, taking flight', *Sydney Morning Herald*, 25 October 2003.

Kevin Rawlinson, 'George Galloway investigated by police for saying Bradford an "Israel-free zone"', *Guardian*, 7 August 2014.

Stuart Rees, 'A craven approach to peace and justice', *Sydney Morning Herald*, 22 October 2013.

Stuart Rees, 'Defending the right to dissent', *New Matilda*, 12 August 2013.

Stuart Rees, 'The Israel lobby's goal is silence', *New Matilda*, 15 April 2014.

Stuart Rees, 'Truth, justice, peace: The moral and legal foundations of the BDS movement', *ABC Religion and Ethics*, 20 November 2013.

David Remnick, 'The One-State Reality', *The New Yorker*, 17 November 2013.

Lee Rhiannon, 'Adjournment speech: Ceasing Australian military co-operation with Israel', *Hansard Senate*, 4 December 2013.

Dave Rich, 'Campus War 1977: The year that Jewish societies were banned', in Alvin H Rosenfeld (ed.), *Resurgent Antisemitism*, Indiana University Press, Bloomington, 2013, pp. 255–76.

Sigmund Roos, Ralph Hexter and Aaron Berman, 'Correction of Misinformation Regarding Trustees' Actions on College Investments', *Hampshire College News*, 12 February 2009.

Hilary Rose and Steven Rose, 'The choice is to do nothing or try to bring about change', *Guardian*, 15 July 2002.

Steven Rosen, 'A European Boycott of Israel?', *Middle East Quarterly*, vol. 21, no. 2, Spring 2014.

David Rosenberg, 'Don't Buy the Israel Boycott Hype', *Wall Street Journal Europe*, 27 February 2014.

MJ Rosenberg, 'The official goal of BDS is ending Israel, not just the '67 occupation', *Tikkun Daily*, 26 March 2014.

Nick Rowbotham, 'Union backs away from BDS motion', *New Matilda*, 6 June 2014.

WD Rubinstein, *The Jews in Australia: A Thematic History, Volume Two*, William Heinemann Australia, Melbourne, 1991.

Laurent Rucker, *Moscow's Surprise: The Soviet-Israeli Alliance of 1947-1949*, Woodrow Wilson International Center for Scholars, Washington, 2005.

Josh Ruebner, *Shattered Hopes: The Failure of Obama's Middle East Peace Process*, Verso, London, 2013.

Samah Sabawi, 'A Palestinian woman's response to Israel's Naomi Chazan on BDS', *Mondoweiss*, 28 July 2011.

Steven Salaita, 'Ten things we've learned about opposition to academic boycott', *Electronic Intifada*, 14 January 2014.

Sol Salbe, 'AJDS endorses nuanced version of BDS', *AJDS Newsletter*, vol. 11, no. 7, 2010, p. 3.

Sol Salbe, 'The AJDS responds to the Jewish Community Council of Victoria', September/October 2010, www.docstoc.com/docs/83434914/Newsletter-September-October-2010, p. 3.

Bibliography

Imre Salusinzky, 'Israeli boycott debate splits state's Greens', *The Australian*, 16 September 2011.

Imre Salusinzky, 'Palestinian consul rejects BDS violence', *The Australian*, 26 October 2011.

Imre Salusinszky and Leo Shanahan, 'Boycott call cost Greens state seat', *The Australian*, 15 April 2011.

Leonard Saxe, Theodore Sasson, Shahar Hecht and Benjamin Phillips, *Still Connected: American Jewish Attitudes about Israel*, Brandeis University, 2010.

Scholars for Peace in the Middle East, *BDS Monitor*, 28 December 2013; 31 January 2014; 28 February 2014.

Scottish Trades Union Congress, 'Supporting Palestinians Boycott Disinvestment & Sanctions Campaign Pack', www.stuc.org.uk/files/Palestine/BDS%20Document.pdf.

Kirk Semple and Gersh Kuntzmann, 'Food Co-op Rejects Effort to Boycott Israeli-Made Products', *New York Times*, 27 March 2012.

Leo Shanahan, 'Anti-Jew protest condemned', *The Australian*, 28 July.

Leo Shanahan, 'Greens boycott rebounds', *The Australian*, 19 April 2011.

Leo Shanahan and Paul Maley, 'Israel boycott anger grows', *The Australian*, 16 April 2011.

Yoram Shapira, 'External and Internal Influences in Latin American-Israeli Relations', in Michael Curtis and Susan Aurelia Gitelson (eds), *Israel in the Third World*, Transaction Books, New Brunswick, 1976.

Ari Shavit, *My Promised Land: the Triumph and Tragedy of Israel*, Scribe, Melbourne, 2014.

Hillel Shenker, 'What's Wrong with BDS?', *Palestine-Israel Journal*, vol. 18, nos. 2 and 3, 2012.

Jonah Shepp, 'Why we Jews get so worked up over BDS', 24 December 2013, www.blog.partners4israel.org/2013/12/why-we-jews-get-so-worked-up-over-bds_24.html.

Dean Sherr, 'Boycott boon to Israel' Right', *The Australian*, 5 November 2013.

Harriet Sherwood, 'Mahmoud Abbas accused of being traitor over rejection of Israel boycott', *Guardian*, 22 December 2013.

Colin Shindler, 'Old Lefts for New: Nye Bevan and Zion', *Jewish Quarterly*, vol. 32, no. 2, 1985, pp. 22–26.

Louis Shub, *The New Left and Israel*, Center for the Study of Contemporary Jewish Life, Los Angeles, 1971.

Maya Shwayder, '134 members of US Congress denounce ASA's Israel boycott', *Jerusalem Post*, 19 January 2014.

Jordy Silverstein, 'What are the possibilities of Jewish/Palestinian solidarity?', 24 June 2013. www.ajds.org.au/jewishpalestiniansolidarity/.

Peter Slezak, 'Anti-Semitism and BDS; Beyond misrepresentations', *ABC Religion and Ethics*, 15 November 2013.

David Speers, 'The Nation', *Sky News*, 14 April 2011.

Jakob Stern, 'Review of T Herzl's book *Der Judenstaat. Versuch einer Losung der Judenfrage*', *Die Neue Zeit*, vol. 15, no. 1, 1896–97, p. 186.

Cameron Stewart, 'Anti-Israel bullies' hard centre bites in chocolate shop campaign', *The Australian*, 20 August 2011.

Larry Stillman, 'AJDS criticizes disruptive BDS protests', 8 September 2011, email newsletter delivered via info@ajds.org.au.

Students for Justice in Palestine, 'Hampshire College becomes first college in U.S. to divest from Israeli Occupation!', 11 February 2009, www.pacbi.org/etemplate.php?id=930.

Pierre-Andre, Taguieff, *Rising from the Muck: The New Anti-Semitism in Europe*, Ivan R Dee, Chicago, 2004.

GH Talhami, *Palestinian Refugees: Pawns to political actors*, Nova Science Publishers, New York, 2003.

Lisa Taraki, 'Palestinian academics call for international academic boycott of Israel', *Birzeit University Right To Education Campaign Activism News*, 7 July 2004.

Matthew Taylor, 'Vote ends Israeli boycott', *Guardian*, 27 May 2005.

The Methodist Church in Britain, 'Methodist boycott of Israeli illegal settlements', London, 2010, www.methodist.org.uk/who-we-are/views-of-the-church/methodist-boycott-of-goods-from-illegal-israeli-settlements.

David Toube, 'The real motive of the boycotters', *Jewish Chronicle*, 21 February 2008.

Jo Tovey, 'Greens abandon official support for Israel boycott', *Sydney Morning Herald*, 5 December 2011.

Enzo Traverso, *The Marxists and the Jewish Question*, Humanities Press, New Jersey, 1994.

Desmond Tutu, 'Israel: time to divest', *New Internationalist*, no. 353, 2003.

University of Haifa, 'The University of Haifa Response to the AUT Decision', 1 May 2005, www.boycottnews.haifa.ac.il/html/html_eng/response_f.htm.

US Campaign to end the Israeli Occupation, *The Palestinian Right of Return*, Washington DC, 2013.

Emile Vandervelde, *Le Pays d'Israel. Un Marxiste en Palestine*, F Rieder, Paris, 1929.

Victorian Trades Hall Council, 'Victorian Trades Hall supports BDS and condemn arrests of Max Brenner 19', 31 August 2011.

Vacy Vlazna, 'Wherefore by their friends ye shall know them: Zionists vs UNSW BDS', *Palestine Chronicle*, 7 May 2013.

Leslie Wagner, 'Watching the Pro-Israeli Academic Watchers', *Jewish Political Studies Review*, vol. 23, no. 12, 15 November 2010.

Kenyon Wallace, 'Ryan rebuked by national CUPE head', *The Star*, 14 January 2009.

Bibliography

Martin A Weiss, *Arab League Boycott of Israel*, Congressional Research Service, Washington, 2013.

Peter Wertheim, *BDS suffers a defeat in Australia: The Marrickville Council Controversy*, Executive Council of Australian Jewry, Sydney, 2011.

Peter Wertheim, *Executive Council of Australian Jewry Annual Report* (2013), Executive Council of Australian Jewry, Sydney, 2013.

Peter Wertheim and Alex Ryvchin, *The Boycott, Divestment and Sanctions (BDS) Campaign against Israel*, Executive Council of Australian Jewry, Sydney, 2014.

Peter Wertheim and Julie Nathan, 'The ugly face of student activism', *The Australian*, 30 April 2013.

Martin Williams, 'Sainsbury's removes kosher food from shelves amid fears over protesters', *Guardian*, 18 August 2014.

Robert Wistrich, 'A deadly mutation: Antisemitism and Anti-Zionism in Great Britain', in Eunice Pollack (ed.), *Antisemitism on the Campus: Past & Present*, Academic Studies Press, Boston, 2011, pp. 53–74.

Robert Wistrich, 'Marxism and Jewish Nationalism: The Theoretical Roots of Confrontation', in Robert Wistrich (ed.), *The Left Against Zion*, Valentine Mitchell, London, 1979.

Adam Withnall, 'George Galloway declares Bradford an Israel-free zone and warns away Israeli tourists', *Independent*, 7 August 2014.

Adam Withnall, 'Sports Direct security guard allegedly banned Jewish schoolboys and told them: "No Jews, no Jews"', *Independent*, 16 September 2014.

World Council of Churches, 'Statement on Israeli settlements in the Occupied Palestinian Territory', 2 September 2009, www.oikoumene.org/en/resources/documents/central-committee/2009/report-on-public-issues/statement-on-israeli-settlements-in-the-occupied-palestinian-territory.

Hicham Yezza, 'Noam Chomsky interviewed by Hicham Yezza', *Ceasefire*, September 22, 2010.

Merav Yudilovitch, 'European magazine demands ideological purity', *Ynetnews*, 22 March 2006.

Michael Yudkin, 'Is an academic boycott of Israel justified?', *Engage Journal*, April 2007, pp. 1–10.

Michael Zakim, 'The Israel Boycott Is Working—to Prevent Peace', *The Chronicle of Higher Education*, 20 October 2014.

Richard Ziegler, *The cults of Bosnia and Palestine*, Baico Publishing, Ottawa, 2012.

Barney Zwartz, 'Christians, Jews meet on boycott', *The Age*, 17 August 2010.

Harold Zwier, 'Why I resigned from the AJDS Executive', *AJDS Newsletter*, vol. 11, no. 8, 2010, p. 4.

Index

Index

Index